ASEAN-Russia Relations

ASEAN-Russia Relations

EDITED BY
Gennady Chufrin • **Mark Hong** • **Teo Kah Beng**

LSEAS

Institute of Southeast Asian Studies
Singapore

IMEMO
Institute of World Economy and International Relations
Russia

First published in Singapore in 2006 by ISEAS Publications
Institute of Southeast Asian Studies
30 Heng Mui Keng Terrace
Pasir Panjang
Singapore 119614

E-mail: publish@iseas.edu.sg
Website: <http://bookshop.iseas.edu.sg>

The responsibility for facts and opinions in this publication rests exclusively with the authors and their interpretations do not necessarily reflect the views or the policy of the publisher or its supporters.

ISEAS Library Cataloguing-in-Publication Data

ASEAN-Russia relations / edited by Gennady Chufrin, Mark Hong, Teo Kah Beng.
   "… the result of a joint conference organized in March 2005 by IMEMO (Institute of World Economy and Politics) and ISEAS (Institute of Southeast Asian Studies) in Singapore"—Foreword.
1.   ASEAN—Congresses.
2.   Southeast Asia—Foreign relations—Russia—Congresses.
3.   Russia—Foreign relations—Southeast Asia—Congresses.
4.   Terrorism—Southeast Asia—Congresses.
5.   National security—Southeast Asia—Congresses.
6.   Southeast Asia—Foreign economic relations—Russia—Congresses.
7.   Russia—Foreign economic relations—Southeast Asia—Congresses.
I.   Chufrin, Gennadl_Illarionovich.
II.   Hong, Mark.
III.   Teo, Kah Beng.
IV.   Institut mirovogo khozia_stva i mirovo_politiki (Akademiia nauk SSSR)
V.   Institute of Southeast Asian Studies.
DS528.8 R9A84   2006

ISBN 981-230-359-6

Typeset by Superskill Graphics Pte Ltd
Printed in Singapore by Seng Lee Press Pte Ltd

Contents

Foreword

This timely book is the result of a joint conference organized in March 2005 by the IMEMO (Institute of World Economy and Politics) and ISEAS (Institute of Southeast Asian Studies) in Singapore. With the rise of India and China, the entire Asian continent is feeling the great impact of socioeconomic changes and challenges created by these twin engines of progress and cooperation. The question on the minds of regional analysts is: Where is Russia in the midst of these vast changes? What is its role?

ASEAN itself is caught up in these challenges. It has responded by a series of initiatives, such as its ambitious vision to build three ASEAN Communities (economic, sociocultural, and security); its forward-looking ASEAN+3 efforts; its proposed Free Trade Agreements with all Asian neighbours, ranging from India, China, Japan, South Korea, and further afield, with the United States and Australia. Individual ASEAN members have contributed greatly, such as Thailand's Asia Cooperation Dialogue; BIMSTEC; the Irrawady-Chao Praya-Mekong Scheme; whilst Singapore has organized the Asia-Middle East Dialogue and the Shangri-La Security Forum; Malaysia has its East Asia Summit; Indonesia has revived the Bandung spirit of cooperation between Africa and Asia; Vietnam is reaching out to the United States. Both India and China are reaching out to ASEAN with several major economic and security initiatives. All these initiatives demonstrate that the region is actively responding to the ferment of the post-Cold War era/post-9/11 challenges.

Russia is now stirring; one good example is its current interest to join the East Asia summit meeting in Kuala Lumpur in December 2005. We in ISEAS set out to explore this intriguing question: how a Great Power like Russia could play an active role in the region, and in what ways ASEAN could engage Russia. Currently, Russia's interaction with ASEAN is limited to the full dialogue between both parties, and trade between both sides is categorized by Russian arms sales and ASEAN raw materials. This book sets out to examine these challenges and opportunities, by examining the state of relations between Russia and selected individual ASEAN countries. This exploration has just started and will continue through a series of conferences, hosted alternately by IMEMO and ISEAS. Several interesting ideas are offered, such as a proposal for a Russia-ASEAN FTA; building tourism/business bridges through budget airlines; proposals to strengthen and energize the ASEAN-Russia dialogue.

It is with the aim of promoting a constructive dialogue between ASEAN and Russia, and the world at large, that this book has been published. I take this opportunity to thank our colleagues in IMEMO and ISEAS, who collectively have helped to launch a worthwhile and challenging endeavour. In particular, I wish to express my appreciation to Mark Hong, Teo Kah Beng and ISEAS Intern Stasia Kostetskaia for their diligent editorial work.

K. Kesavapany
Director
Institute of Southeast Asian Studies
Singapore
14 September 2005

Foreword

This conference organized by the ISEAS undoubtedly presents an important landmark in relations between academic communities of Russia and the ASEAN countries. Moreover the mere fact of holding this conference reflects a growing interest between our countries, our societies in promoting more close and mutually beneficial relationship on a wide range of issues — political, economic, cultural.

It is worth noting in this regard that the ISEAS-IMEMO conference is organized on the eve of the first Russia-ASEAN Summit which is to be held later this year. And it is quite logical therefore that the conference agenda addresses most crucial political, economic and security problems that evoke mutual interest and concern. I wish that conference participants will concentrate not only on analysing these problems but may work out concrete recommendations to our respective governments, academic and business communities on strengthening and broadening our cooperation.

Russia now pursues an ambitious national development strategy going far beyond resolution of economic and social problems it inherited from the previous times. In fact, the strategy is aimed at laying a solid foundation for a sustained progress of Russia as a democratic and prosperous country ready to cooperate with other nations. While pursuing these goals, Russia is particularly interested in promoting cooperation with the countries of East and Southeast Asia. For these purposes, Russia intends to use its considerable potential of human, industrial and natural resources as well as to take an active part in the now strengthening regional cooperation in East Asia. It also believes that in the process of such cooperation with regional countries on a bilateral as well as multilateral basis, the development of its own regions of Siberia and the Far East will be greatly facilitated.

I sincerely hope that the forthcoming discussions at our conference covering these and other issues of the Russia-ASEAN relationship will be both thought provoking and intellectually rewarding.

Professor Gennady Chufrin
Deputy Director
Institute of World Economy and
International Relations (IMEMO)
Russia

Opening Address

Today we launch the inaugural seminar of the IMEMO-ISEAS series, with this timely meeting, which focuses on ASEAN-Russia relations. Many great changes are underway in the Asia-Pacific, such as the recent developments in North Korea and Taiwan-China, as well as evolving trends in the trilateral U.S.-Japan-China relations. Russia is both participant, as in the Six-Party Talks on North Korea, as well as a keen observer of regional trends. ASEAN itself is bound to be affected by these regional developments. It is therefore useful and timely for both sides to exchange views and perceptions on topics of mutual interests.

Beyond these considerations, Russia is an ASEAN dialogue partner and will also take part in the ASEAN Summit to be held in 2005. This seminar, as well as the next leg to be held in Moscow in 2006 and hosted by IMEMO, provides an opportunity for the exchange of ideas and inputs into the ASEAN Summit process. As bilateral relations are an integral part of the dialogue process, it is also relevant to discuss Russia's relations with key ASEAN countries, such as Indonesia, Malaysia and Singapore. Papers on these aspects will be presented at this seminar.

On bilateral relations, there is renewed interest on the part of Singapore companies in the Russian market. Both Russia and Singapore are key players in the Asia-Pacific energy markets, Russia as a growing supplier of oil and gas to the North Pacific markets, and Singapore as a key oil refiner, trader and market price setter. Energy issues might form a suitable area of discussions in future seminars in this series.

There have been a growing number of exchange visits of trade and business delegations as well as parliamentary delegations between both sides. Such contacts help to strengthen relations and help to increase knowledge about business opportunities in Russia, which is a fast growing economy with solid growth prospects. Academic connections will enhance mutual understanding and also help to further strengthen growing ties and expand networking contacts.

I would like to also take this opportunity to thank H.E. Ambassador of the Russian Federation, Mr. Sergei Kiselev, Professor Gennady Chufrin of IMEMO, IE Singapore and Amtel Company for their invaluable support for this seminar. We all look forward to fruitful discussions at this seminar and a productive collaboration with IMEMO in the future.

K. Kesavapany
Director
Institute of Southeast Asian Studies

Opening Address

It is my great pleasure to be invited today and to be given an opportunity to address you on the occasion of a seminar jointly organized by the Institute of Southeast Asian Studies (ISEAS) and Russian Academy of Sciences' Institute of the World Economy and International Relations (IMEMO). I am not flattering anyone when I state that these two famous institutions represent what may be the sharpest minds of two nations and always tend to be at the research edge in their never-ending academic quest.

The theme of the seminar, "ASEAN Relations with Russia", covers a wide range of topics to be discussed and proves a great deal of mutual interest existing both in my home country and within the region of Southeast Asia — home base for ASEAN members. I shall talk briefly from the Russian angle and try to define why Russia is interested in deepening its relations with ASEAN and why the association might be interested in Russia as well.

In the era of increasing globalization and technical innovation, what lies beneath our mutual interest in each other? It is not only geographical factor that two-thirds of Russia's territory belongs to the Asian region making it the biggest Euro-Asian country in the world. As the case of Singapore proves, size matters, but it is not crucial to success. It is not a matter of rich variety of natural resources — Singapore again sets up an excellent example that even without a drop of its own oil it is possible to become one of the biggest oil refiners globally.

We are living in a constantly and rapidly changing environment to which we have to adapt flexibly in order to survive and prosper. In this small and highly interdependent world we face the same challenges and depend on each other more and more. I am not saying that we are similar; we have a lot of differences — historical, political, and cultural. Yet we share the same values

— we help when someone cries out for our help, like it was in tsunami-hit Aceh, Thailand and Sri Lanka. We stay united and determined, when attacked by the terror.

I am fully convinced that besides all other important factors, these alone could serve as a solid foundation for our widening relations. I am sure that forthcoming discussions, timely and topical, will shed more light on the substance of the subject.

Russia sees ASEAN as an authoritative and influential organization which actively assists the integration processes in the Asia-Pacific region. Russia highly values the constructive role that ASEAN plays in ensuring stability in Southeast Asia, in its economic and social development.

ASEAN has gained a strong foothold as one of the major centres of influence in the Asia-Pacific region, become a unique "nucleus" of regional integration processes and a gravitational field both for Asian and non-regional states. Development of diversified links with ASEAN is a priority area of Russian policy in Asia. We constantly confirm that in word and deed.

We appreciate ASEAN's philosophy of multilateral interaction, its firm commitment to the UN Charter, settlement of disputes by political methods. The recent accession of Russia to the Bali Treaty of 1976, which for almost three decades has been a solid foundation for peace in Southeast Asia and the Asia-Pacific region as a whole, is a telling proof of that.

ASEAN and Russia have similar approaches to major global and regional problems. We collaborate closer and closer in multilateral associations, the foremost example being within the framework of the ASEAN Regional Forum (ARF). Our partnership is becoming an increasingly influential factor for ensuring peace and stability in the Asia-Pacific region.

Political dialogue with the association provides a basis for developing cooperation in the areas of economy, science and technology, tourism, culture and education. We are ready to work on various joint projects with ASEAN partners.

The last two years have witnessed a qualitative breakthrough in our relations. The regulatory and legal frameworks of Russia-ASEAN relations are being intensively developed. The ASEAN-Russia Joint Declaration on Partnership for Peace and Security, Prosperity and Development in the Asia Pacific, which serves as the main framework for further build-up of relations with the association, was signed in Phnom Penh in June 2003. The Joint Declaration for Cooperation to Combat International Terrorism, which made it possible to start developing practical counter-terrorism interaction, was signed in Jakarta in 2004. The next item on the agenda is an agreement on economic cooperation, which we expect to be signed during the ASEAN-Russia ministerial meeting in Laos in July 2005.

Interaction with ASEAN is particularly significant for Russia in terms of achieving our social and economic objectives, developing Siberia and the Far East regions and promoting the well-being of Russian citizens. Practical interaction with Russia in the fields of high technologies, science, energy, culture, tourism, etc., is also particularly beneficial for ASEAN.

The accumulated potential of ASEAN-Russia ties makes it possible to bring them to the highest level. We are convinced that the first ASEAN-Russia Summit to be held in December 2005 will become a genuine landmark and give a powerful impetus to developing dynamic and mutually beneficial relations.

Dramatic shifts in the ASEAN-Russia relations have become possible due to close interactions between all parties involved that specifically underlines the role of Singapore as the coordinator for the ASEAN-Russia dialogue. We are grateful to the Republic for its endless efforts in this direction and treasure our long-standing friendly relations, which have undergone major changes in nature since their establishment back in 1968.

Political dialogue with Singapore, which is considered by Russia as one of the key players in the region, has been developing on a steady path in recent years. Following respective exchange of visits by Singaporean and Russian foreign ministers in 2002 and 2003, last year witnessed an important visit by George Yeo, then Minister for Trade and Industry, at the helm of a business delegation to Moscow and Saint Petersburg. More high profile visits are on the agenda of bilateral contacts. Besides, we have a regular inter-ministerial dialogue in the form of bilateral consultations at the level of deputy foreign ministers and directors of political departments, as well as constructive and productive interaction at various levels in international organizations. We have a good mutual understanding and share similar approaches to many issues.

Political dialogue is important. The key to development of bilateral ties is closer cooperation in trade, investment and technology. Trade figures are somewhat comforting. In 2004, total turnover surged by more than 30 per cent on a year-on-year basis and amounted to US$696.5 million, with Russian exports totalling US$322.6 million, and imports totalling US$373.9 million. There is spacious room for improvement. From our point of view, trade structure needs more diversity as well — energy-related unprocessed items coupled with ferrous and non-ferrous metals now account for more than 80 per cent of total Russian exports to Singapore. We do not underestimate the importance of the resource-oriented trading. We would like to see more bilateral cooperation in such advanced fields as biomedicine, engineering and electronics, IT technologies and software development.

Russia has inherited and developed a solid research and development base, globally renowned school of fundamental science, highly skilled and professional staff. Take any field of advanced research and you will find Russian names in the list, be it space, lasers, informatics, bio and chemical technologies, pharmacology, radioelectronics, defence and dual technologies, etc. This potential could and should be widely utilized in collaboration with ASEAN members, including Singapore, in transforming their largely industrial economy to one based upon fundamental research and exclusive knowledge.

Singapore is widely referred to as a regional hub — in trade and industry, finance and investment, transport and communication. Vast opportunities for bilateral interaction in developing it into an advanced technology hub are also present. We are determined to further deepen cooperation between universities and research centres. Russia could learn from Singapore's experience in the commercialization of science and technology.

The first steps have been taken. Russia stays in the focus of the Singapore Government agencies and business organizations: Besides a major agreement on double-taxation in 2002, protocols and MOUs were signed in 2002 and 2003 respectively between the Russian Union of Industrialists and Entrepreneurs and the Singapore Confederation of Industries, the Russian Chamber of Commerce and Industry and IE Singapore. A delegation of the association of Small and Medium enterprises "OPORA of Russia" visited Singapore on the occasion of "Global Entrepolis Singapore" in October 2004 and signed an MOU with the Singapore Business Federation. Singapore agreed to support Russia's accession to the WTO, which is very important for us. There are several bilateral agreements currently being discussed and shaped up, including an investment guarantees agreement, on science and technology cooperation and a visa waiving agreement.

Singapore is considered as a "Go Ahead!" light for many Asian Investors. If Singaporeans make their move, for the rest of the region it means that it is safe and promising to follow them. We welcome more visible presence of Singaporean companies in the Russian market, which in turn will result in broader cooperation between Russia and other countries of ASEAN. This will also create a backstream of Russian companies to Singapore and the region. The current level of mutual investments cannot satisfy both sides: Singaporean investments in Russia from 1999 to 2002 amount to a mere US\$160 million (for comparison — Russian investments in Singapore stand at US\$62.5 million). According to other data, accumulated Singapore investments in

Russia since the beginning of the 1990s to 2003 could amount up to US$770 million. But this is still below the potential. The idea of establishing a Russia-Singapore investment fund is timely and certainly deserves greater attention. It is very encouraging that such Singaporean corporate "giants" like "Singapore Technologies" and "Temasek Holdings" are showing strong interest in the Russian market.

Another direction of our bilateral cooperation could be Singaporean participation in large-scale projects with the regional dimension undertaken by Russia in the areas of energy, transportation, and telecommunications.

These are my brief insights on this long-term subject. I am confident that this seminar will mark a beginning of a series of bilateral academic exchanges in the fields which are undoubtedly much needed by both sides.

I would like to thank all organizers of this important event, participating members from ISEAS and IMEMO and personally Director Kesavapany and Deputy Director Chufrin, for their interest and efforts and wish this seminar and its participants every success.

Sergey B. Kiselev
Ambassador Extraordinary and Plenipotentiary
of the Russian Federation

The Contributors

Viacheslav B. AMIROV is currently Senior Research Fellow, Center for Japanese and Pacific Studies, IMEMO. He graduated from Moscow State University (Economics Faculty) in 1971, and joined IMEMO in 1971 where he received his Ph.D. in Economics in 1975. Amirov has written numerous articles about Russia's role and relations in the Asia-Pacific region. His professional interests include Russia's relations with Asia-Pacific countries, economic integration in East Asia, and the roles of Japan and the United States in the region.

AW Siew Juan is currently the Director of International Operations (Europe) and Enterprise Group of International Enterprise Singapore, or IE Singapore (formerly known as the Trade Development Board). Aw joined IE Singapore in 1986 and started her career in trade policy work. She graduated with an Honours degree in Social Science from the National University of Singapore. She was awarded a Raffles Scholarship to pursue a one-year Master's programme at the University of Warwick where she graduated with an M.A. in International Political Economy in 1995.

Gennady CHUFRIN is Deputy Director, Institute of World Economy and International Relations (IMEMO), Russian Academy of Sciences, Moscow. He is author/co-author of fifteen monographs and over 120 articles published both in Russia and abroad, in Russian, English, French, Japanese, Korean and Tajik, on international security, Russian foreign policy issues as well as the Asia-Pacific region. He graduated from the Leningrad State University in 1958 and received a Ph.D. in international economics in 1965 from the same university. In 1981, he received a Professor's degree in international economics from the Institute of Oriental Studies, Russian Academy of Sciences. In 1994, he was elected as Associate Member of the Russian Academy of Sciences; in 1995 he was Lombard Fellow at the Kettering Foundation (U.S.); and in 1996, became Distinguished Fellow at CSIS, Jakarta. Chufrin has worked in various capacities as diplomat, official and academic in Indonesia, India, Pakistan, and Sweden (SIPRI) before assuming his present post in 2002.

Mark HONG Tat Soon was awarded the President of the Republic of Singapore's Scholarship in 1965. He obtained a B.A. in Economics from Cambridge University in 1969 and an M.Sc. in International Relations from Georgetown University in Washington, D.C. in 1982 on a Fulbright Scholarship. He joined the Ministry of Foreign Affairs in 1969. He served at the Singapore foreign missions in Phnom Penh, Hong Kong, Paris, and at the Singapore Permanent Mission to the UN in New York. His last foreign posting was as Singapore Ambassador to Russia and Ukraine from November 1995 to March 2002. He has since been attached to the Institute of Defence and Strategic Studies, Nanyang Technological University, Singapore, as a visiting senior fellow. He is currently a Vice-Chairman of the International Committee of the Singapore Business Federation, an International Advisor to the Port of Singapore Authority, and a Visiting Research Fellow at ISEAS. He has delivered over a hundred conference papers and lectures to various international seminars and conferences.

Sidney JONES has been the Southeast Asia Project Director of the International Crisis Group (ICG) since May 2002 and is presently also Visiting Fellow at ISEAS. Before assuming her appointment with ICG she spent fourteen years as Asia Director of Human Rights Watch. Jones' expertise is on Indonesia, terrorism in Southeast Asia and Islam in Southeast Asia. As Southeast Asia Project Director of ICG she has worked on the sources of conflict and violence in the region, with particular focus on Indonesia. She has examined separatist conflicts (Aceh, Papua, and Mindanao), communal conflicts (Poso, Moluccas), and ethnic conflict (Kalimantan). She and her team have also worked on Islamic radicalism, producing a series of reports on the Jemaah Islamiyah and its operations in Indonesia and the Philippines. Jones frequently briefs the media, international organizations, and government representatives and has written extensively on these issues.

K. S. NATHAN holds a B.A. Hons. in History from the University of Malaya; Ph.D. in International Relations from Claremont Graduate University in California; LL.B. Hons. from the University of London, Certificate in Legal Practice (CLP) Malaysia, and LL.M. from the University of London. He taught International Relations at the Department of History, University of

Malaya. He is currently Senior Fellow at ISEAS. Nathan has held several Visiting Fellowships, including at Harvard University, USSR Academy of Sciences, London School of Economics, and Australian National University. He is also the current President of the Malaysian Association for American Studies (MAAS), and serves on the Editorial Board of the *Australian Journal of International Affairs*. Since January 2003, he has been Editor of the ISEAS journal *Contemporary Southeast Asia*. His latest publications include two edited works entitled, *The European Union, United States and ASEAN: Challenges and Prospects for Cooperative Engagement in the 21st Century* (2002), and *Islam in Southeast Asia: Political, Social and Strategic Challenges for the 21st Century* (2005). He has also published numerous articles in local, regional, and international journals. His teaching, research, and publications are largely in the area of strategic studies, big power relations in the Asia-Pacific region, ASEAN regionalism, and Malaysian politics and foreign policy, and more recently, political Islam, terrorism, and regional security.

Rahul SEN is a Fellow in Regional Economic Studies programme at the Institute of Southeast Asian Studies (ISEAS), Singapore. He earned his Masters degree in Economics from the Delhi School of Economics, India in 1996, and his PhD degree from the Department of Economics, National University of Singapore in 2003. His research interests are mainly in the area of International Trade and Investment in the Asia-Pacific region, focusing on regionalism. His current area of research is regional trade policy issues in Asia. He has published and co-authored numerous papers related to Free Trade Agreements involving Singapore and other Asian economies. At ISEAS, Dr. Sen is also one of the co-editors of the regional journal, *ASEAN Economic Bulletin*, and is a member of the Trade Policy Unit that focuses on policy-oriented research on trade policy issues involving Southeast Asian economies.

Rodolfo C. SEVERINO is a Visiting Senior Research Fellow at ISEAS. Having been Secretary-General of the Association of Southeast Asian Nations from 1998 to 2002, he is working on a book on issues facing ASEAN, including the economic, security and other challenges confronting the region. His views on ASEAN and Southeast Asia have been published in *ASEAN Today and Tomorrow*, a compilation of his speeches and other statements. As a member of the faculty at the Asian Institute of Management in the Philippines in the school year 2003–04, he lectured on regional economic cooperation, the elements of competitiveness, and leadership in the management of change. Before assuming the position of ASEAN Secretary-General, Severino was Undersecretary of Foreign Affairs of the Philippines. In the Philippine Foreign Service, Severino served in Malaysia,

Beijing, Houston, Texas, and in Washington, D.C. He has a B.A. degree in the humanities from Ateneo de Manila University and an M.A. degree in international relations from the Johns Hopkins University School of Advanced International Studies.

Victor SUMSKY is Head of Section, Center for Development and Modernization Studies, IMEMO, Russian Academy of Sciences. He has written three monographs and has co-authored/contributed to twelve books. Sumsky graduated from the Moscow State Institute for International Relations (MGIMO) in 1975, and received a Ph.D. from the Institute of Oriental Studies, USSR Academy of Sciences in 1983. He speaks Russian, English and Indonesian, and has worked in the Soviet Foreign Ministry, Institute of Oriental Studies and is currently at IMEMO. His overseas working experience includes the University of the Philippines, London School of Economics, and the University of Washington. His areas of professional interests include the political development of ASEAN countries, and security and international relations in the Asia-Pacific region.

Leo SURYADINATA is Senior Research Fellow at ISEAS. He was formerly Professor of Political Science at the National University of Singapore. He has published extensively on ethnic Chinese in Southeast Asia as well as China-ASEAN relations. His books include: *China and the ASEAN States: Ethnic Chinese Dimension* (1985), *Pribumi Indonesian, the Chinese Minority and China* (1993, third edition) and *Ethnic Relations and Nation-Building in Southeast Asia: The Case of the Ethnic Chinese* (editor and contributor, 2004).

Andrew T. H. TAN is Assistant Professor, Institute of Defence and Strategic Studies, Nanyang Technological University, Singapore. His latest books include *Security Perspectives of the Malay Archipelago: Security Linkages in the Second Front in the War on Terrorism* (2004) and *A Political and Economic Dictionary of South-East Asia* (2004). A graduate of Cambridge and Sydney universities, Andrew specializes in Southeast Asian security and terrorism. His forthcoming books include *The Politics of Terrorism* and *A Handbook of Terrorism and Insurgency in Southeast Asia*.

TEO Kah Beng is a Ph.D. candidate (Political Science) at the National University of Singapore. He obtained an M.A. (International Relations) degree from the Australian National University. He is currently an Associate Lecturer (International Relations) at the Singapore Institute of Management, and a part-time Tutor at the Nanyang Technological University.

PART I
Overview of ASEAN-Russia Relations

1
ASEAN Engages Russia

Rodolfo C. Severino

This chapter seeks to present the Association of Southeast Asian Nations'
perspectives on Russia — that is, the perspectives of ASEAN as a group —
within the context of the relations between Russia and, again, ASEAN as a
group. I will not deal with the perspectives on or the relations with Russia of
individual ASEAN members, although those perspectives and relations help
shape those of ASEAN as a group and the other way around.

ASEAN's relations with Russia are anchored on:

- The "dialogue" relationship;
- The ASEAN Regional Forum;
- The senior officials consultations;
- The Joint Cooperation Committee;
- Science and technology linkages; and, now,
- The ASEAN-Russia Summit Meeting scheduled in Kuala Lumpur in
  December 2005.

During the Cold War, the ASEAN countries recognized the Soviet Union
as a superpower with global reach and significance. Accordingly, by 1976,
most Southeast Asian countries had diplomatic relations with Moscow, after
decades of hesitation and wariness. However, there persisted obstacles to
closer relations with the USSR on the part of ASEAN as a whole and of its
individual members. The Soviet Union's centrally planned economy constituted
a barrier to a thriving economic relationship. The Cold War and geopolitical

considerations engendered mutual suspicions. Vietnam's incursion into Cambodia, starting in late 1978, reinforced ASEAN's suspicions of Moscow, even as those suspicions influenced ASEAN's vehement opposition to Vietnam's move. After all, just before the incursion, Vietnam had joined COMECON and entered into what amounted to a mutual defence treaty with the USSR, whose communist ideology and perceived aggressive stance were regarded by ASEAN members as a threat.

In the late 1980s, several developments conspired to ease the way to improved ASEAN-Soviet relations. Mikhail Gorbachev's *glasnost* and *perestroika* were transforming the Soviet Union's domestic situation and foreign relations. Vietnam completed the withdrawal of its troops from Cambodia in 1989. Soviet support for Vietnam had perceptibly diminished. The peace process on Cambodia was gaining momentum, partly as a result of an apparent Sino-Soviet understanding. There was the larger improvement in Sino-Soviet relations. Finally, the Soviet Union broke up and the Cold War ended.

With the end of the Cold War emerged a new security configuration in East Asia. For ASEAN, it was time for stronger engagement with all major powers that had interests in East Asia and roles to play in the region's security. And, for ASEAN, Moscow, even in its diminished state, had a strategic role to play in East Asia. Like China, Russia was a permanent member of the United Nations Security Council, a recognized nuclear power, and a leading conventional military force.

Thus, at the 1991 ASEAN Ministerial Meeting, Russia and China were both on hand as guests of Malaysia, the host of the meeting. The next year, they were at the meeting in Manila as guests of the chairman of the ASEAN Standing Committee, a notch higher in status. At the January 1992 ASEAN Summit in Singapore, the ASEAN leaders directed the association to use the framework of the Post-Ministerial Conferences (PMC) for dealing with regional security issues.

At the senior officials' meeting of the PMC countries later that year, the ASEAN Regional Forum (ARF) was conceived as a new body for discussing regional security questions. The ARF was to include not only ASEAN and its dialogue partners but also the ASEAN observers — Papua New Guinea and, at that time, Laos and Vietnam — and the then "consultative partners" — Russia and China. Two years after the ARF's inaugural meeting in 1994, Russia, as well as China and India, was taken in as an ASEAN dialogue partner.

Aside from participating in the ASEAN Post-Ministerial Conferences and the ASEAN Regional Forum, Russia engaged ASEAN in political consultations between senior foreign ministry officials. An ASEAN-Russia

Joint Cooperation Committee was formed to manage development cooperation, with a Joint Planning and Management Committee, a working group on trade and economic cooperation, and a working group on science and technology. A working group on tourism has been proposed.

A number of impulses drive ASEAN's relationship with Russia. They do *not* include official development assistance. A US$5-million ASEAN-Russia fund was talked about at the beginning of the dialogue partnership but has not materialized for technical reasons. Nor do ASEAN's motives involve trade at this point. ASEAN-Russia trade in 2003 amounted to less than US$4 billion, a paltry sum in comparison to ASEAN-China trade, which was valued at US$78.2 billion in the same year. However, Russia is promising as a source of tourism. Its scientific and technical advances make partnership with it potentially useful for basic science, applied technology, energy technology, and other areas. Russia is, of course, a leading source of energy, actual or potential, for Western Europe, China and Japan, and could be for ASEAN as well.

It is, however, Russia's standing in the world that makes it important as an ASEAN partner. It is a recognized nuclear-weapon state and a conventional military power. It is a permanent member of the UN Security Council. It belongs to the Group of 8 leading industrial nations. It is the leader of the Commonwealth of Independent States and exerts great influence in Central Asia and the Middle East. It is part of the Quartet engaged in the Israel-Palestine peace process. It is one of the organizers of the Shanghai Cooperation Organization, which forms an added link between Russia and China. Russia takes part in the Six-Party Talks on the nuclear problem in North Korea. It is a vast source of essential raw materials, particularly for energy. It is richly endowed in certain areas of science and technology.

In view of its strategic importance, ASEAN finds it useful to engage in regular political consultations with Moscow at the level of senior officials. Russia specially sent its foreign minister to Vientiane on the occasion of the ASEAN Summit there in November 2004 in order to formalize its accession to the Treaty of Amity and Cooperation in Southeast Asia. China, India, Japan, Pakistan and South Korea had earlier acceded to the treaty. Together with France, the United Kingdom and the United States, Russia is still negotiating with ASEAN the terms of the protocol by which the nuclear-weapon states are to associate themselves with the treaty on the Southeast Asia Nuclear Weapons-Free Zone. ASEAN and Russia issued the Joint Declaration of Foreign Ministers on Partnership for Peace and Security and Prosperity and Development in the Asia-Pacific in June 2003, and the Joint Declaration of Foreign Ministers on Cooperation in Combating International Terrorism in July 2004. Whether these will amount to anything tangible remains to be seen. At the December 2005 ASEAN-Russia Summit, more joint declarations are expected, probably to cover international terrorism, security and economic cooperation. Holding the ASEAN-Russia Summit regularly is being considered, one possibility being once every two years. Russian participation in the East Asia Summit is not being ruled out.

To summarize: In ASEAN's eyes, Russia is a powerful country, a global actor with a constructive role to play in East Asia, particularly in strategic terms and in dealing with international terrorism. Russian and ASEAN markets are still not familiar to each other, though perhaps more so now than in Soviet times. Russia is a valuable energy source. There is much potential for tourism both ways, and ample room for cooperation in science and technology.

ASEAN and Russia consider each other to be important enough to be receptive to regular ASEAN-Russia Summits.

2
Russian Perspectives on ASEAN

Gennady Chufrin

As a Eurasian country Russia — similarly to the former Soviet Union — has strong national interests in Asia in general and in Southeast Asia in particular. They are formed not by mere geography but by a rich variety of political, economic, security, demographic, cultural and other factors. Obviously at different periods of the Soviet/Russian history some of these factors became more prominent than the others thus influencing the choice of national objectives and means of their achievement.

Reflecting fundamental geopolitical changes and new security challenges in the post-Cold War world, Russia's foreign policy in the post-Soviet period became fundamentally different from that of the Soviet times both in its goals and in methods of achieving them. The former great power's assertive goals were replaced with the need to create a favourable external environment for Russia's economic development. And while the Soviet Union's main instruments of pursuing its strategic goals were ideological and military, the new democratic Russia places emphasis on diplomatic and political methods in its foreign policy.

Shortly after Vladimir Putin was elected Russian President in 2000, a revised "National Security Concept" and a new "Foreign Policy Concept" were adopted by him. In both of these documents, economic issues were placed at the centre of the long-term national development strategy. The "Foreign Policy Concept" stated in particular that in order to ensure Russia's national security and to strengthen its sovereignty and territorial integrity, the Russian Government should concentrate on:

a) Creation of favourable external conditions for a progressive economic development of Russia and for a noticeable improvement in the living standards of its population;
b) Formation of a good-neighbourly belt along its national borders, assistance in resolution of existing and prevention of emergence of new tensions and conflicts in areas adjacent to the Russian Federation;
c) Search for common and complementary interests with foreign countries and international organizations while pursuing national priority goals; creation of a system of partnership and alliances on this basis that would facilitate international cooperation.

As a result, not only did Russia's policy become more oriented towards economic issues, but with the passage of time, it also reflected changes in the national economic priorities. If the first post-Soviet decade's development of economic relations with Russia's external partners was heavily motivated by the urgent need to overcome immediate consequences of the breakdown of the Soviet centrally-planned economic system, these concerns were later largely replaced by long-term development considerations. Consequently, promoting economic relations became an important factor in facilitating the overall state of Russia's relations with its regional neighbours in East Asia. Moreover other aspects of post-Soviet Russia's policy in East Asia, including promotion of military security, now became decidedly more oriented towards creating a peaceful and cooperative regional environment contributing to Russia's economic development requirements.

In the post-Soviet period Russia stopped regarding any East or Southeast Asian country as its adversary and declared its intention to develop normal, preferably friendly, relations with all of them. No longer influenced by a global confrontation of two military blocs and by the threat of a nuclear holocaust, the post-communist Russia embarked on a course of reducing its defence budget, the size of its armed forces — including strategic military arsenal — and its military deployments abroad.

In East and Southeast Asia, these fundamental changes resulted in a complete withdrawal of Russian armed forces from Mongolia at the beginning of the 1990s and from Vietnam where the Russian naval base in Cam Ranh Bay was closed down in 2002. It should be noted here that the decision to close down this base was taken two years ahead of a formal expiry of the existing agreement between Russia and Vietnam on its lease. Commenting on this decision, the then Russian Prime Minister Mikhail Kasyanov, while on a state visit in Hanoi in March 2002, said that Russian military presence there "became an outdated method of achieving strategic goals". During the 1990s, Russia also significantly reduced its armed forces on its own eastern territories, that is, in Siberia and the Russian Far East. During this period the ground forces deployed there were cut down from 390,000 to 170,000 servicemen. The number of combat aircraft was reduced from 2,430 to around 900. The Russian Pacific Fleet, once a formidable force capable of competing with the U.S. navy, was radically rolled back in size and firepower. The number of its principal surface combatants was cut down from 100 to 16 while only 21 submarines out of 140 were left in operational service. Also, as a gesture of goodwill towards Japan, Russia withdrew its regular troops from the Southern Kuriles, leaving only border guard units.

During the first decade of the twenty-first century, Russia continued to demonstrate its firm intention to maintain the size of its conventional forces in the eastern part of the country at the level of minimal sufficient security. Also it was considered quite essential to emphasize that Russian national interests in East and Southeast Asia were in no way contradictory to the national interests of regional countries. In fact, they were complementary since post-Soviet Russia did not claim any privileges and did not intend to strengthen its security at someone else's expense or to the detriment of other states.

While diminishing the role of military power in its foreign policy, Russia resolutely shifted the emphasis to political methods of pursuing its national interests both globally and on the regional level. Reflecting the end of bipolarity in international relations after the end of the Cold War and responding to new realities and challenges in the modern world, Russia declared multipolarity to be one of the basic principles of its foreign policy. By this, Russia stated its opposition to building a new world order on the basis of unipolarity and underscored its understanding that a unipolar world cannot adequately reflect the diversity of national interests and concerns of different countries. In fact unipolarity would, in Moscow's opinion, cause international tensions and conflicts. From the Russian perception a multipolar approach to international relations can and should be a more convenient instrument in dealing with different international actors as it takes into account their specific needs and requirements in a constructive and cooperative manner.

Addressing objective realities of international relations both globally and regionally, the policy of multipolarity proved to be particularly effective in East Asia where international relations had in fact been multipolar even during the days of bipolarity and remained such after the end of the Cold

War. Conducting its policy on the principles of multipolarity helped Russia not only to promote its ties with its former friends and allies in East and Southeast Asia (such as Vietnam) but also to upgrade significantly its relations with such important regional actors as China and Japan. Acting in the spirit of multipolarity also allowed Russia to avoid being tied up to any one-sided political or ideological approaches, to have maximum flexibility in dealing with the outside world and to pursue its national interests in a completely pragmatic manner.

Commenting on the principles of multipolarity incorporated in the Russian foreign policy, Igor Ivanov, former Minister of Foreign Affairs and currently Secretary of the National Security Council, wrote:

> We shall conduct our foreign policy proceeding from a firm conviction that the best basis for a stable world order is multipolarity which excludes monopoly or domination of any single power or a group of states in international affairs. Russia is not alone in this approach. It is absolutely clear for us that the majority of nations aspire to establish a global system based on justice and equality. Even those of them who are U.S. allies obviously do not want to accept, least of all to approve, a hegemony of one superpower or one military alliance in world affairs.

Pursuing a multipolar policy should be in no way seen as an attempt by Moscow to create a spirit of confrontation in international affairs. Commenting on its basic principles, Igor Ivanov wrote:

> A world order which is emerging in the twenty-first century presupposes existence of unity in diversity. Pluralism is essential for democracy. Tactical differences in approaches should not cause reduction in efficiency of international cooperation, so much the more to create a danger of a split in structures of regional cooperation existing under the auspices of the UNO and dealing with resolution of essential international problems which are of similar concern to all interested parties.

Promotion of relations with the Association of the Southeast Asian Nations (ASEAN) as one of the most important organizations in East Asia plays a notable role in the Russian foreign policy of multipolarity. With the admission of three Indochinese states and Myanmar into ASEAN in 1995–99 the latter became synonymous with the now unified Southeast Asia. Moreover, it made ASEAN an influential actor in modern international relations far beyond its geographical boundaries.

Under these conditions, annual ASEAN post-ministerial conferences (PMCs) and the ASEAN Regional Forum (ARF) began to be regarded by Moscow as important venues contributing to building up peace and stability not only in East Asia but also in a wider Asia Pacific region. Since the middle of the 1990s Russia became a regular participant in the PMCs as a fully-fledged ASEAN "dialogue partner" and an active member of the ARF. It also established direct dialogue with ASEAN at the level of foreign ministers, which was to serve as a forum for the discussion of political issues of mutual interest on a regular basis. Russia and ASEAN member-states also created a joint cooperation committee with the aim of holding regular meetings on development of economic cooperation as well as on coordination of their struggles against international criminal activities, including international terrorism.

Based on the above principles, Russia's relations with ASEAN on political and security issues have consistently developed in the spirit of growing trust and cooperation. Listed below are major landmarks in the progress of Russia-ASEAN relations over the last few years:

a) Russia fully subscribed to the ASEAN proposal of establishing in Southeast Asia a zone of peace, freedom and neutrality (ZOPFAN), thus supporting an idea of neutralization of Southeast Asia.

b) Since Russia was vitally interested in the non-proliferation of nuclear weapons, it also supported the ASEAN idea of creating a nuclear weapons free zone (SEANWFZ) in Southeast Asia.

c) Since 2001 when the Shanghai Cooperation Organization (SCO) was established, ASEAN and SCO, of which Russia is a prominent member, started to build up closer ties on issues of regional security.

d) In 2003 in Pnom Penh, Russia and ASEAN signed a Joint Declaration on Peace and Security aimed at promoting relations of political partnership on these issues.

e) In July 2004 Russia and ASEAN adopted another Joint Declaration on Cooperation to combat international terrorism which opened a new area of cooperation between them.

f) In the same month the lower chamber of the Russian Parliament (Duma) adopted a federal law sanctioning Russia to join the ASEAN Treaty of Amity and Cooperation (the 1976 Bali Treaty). Following this decision Russia officially joined the Bali Treaty in November 2004 and became its non-regional signatory along with China, Japan, India and Pakistan.

g) This act strengthened significantly political and legal foundations of the Russia-ASEAN relationship and paved the way for the next important step – holding of the first ASEAN-Russia Summit Meeting which is expected to take place at the end of 2005 in Kuala Lumpur.

Russia also declared its support of the fundamental conceptual principles guiding ASEAN into the twenty-first century as they are formulated in the ASEAN Concord II that was adopted at the Ninth ASEAN Summit in October 2003. The proposed ASEAN community to be created by the year 2020 on three "pillars" — ASEAN Security Community, ASEAN Economic Community and ASEAN Socio-Cultural Community — resonates favourably with Russia's own vision of a Pacific Concord proposed by Moscow in 1999. In its proposal Russia suggested to enhance regional security in the Asia-Pacific region by a stage-by-stage progress in regional politics from adoption of confidence-building measures by its member-states to preventive diplomacy and finally to the establishment of conflict resolution mechanisms. These ideas seem to be not dissimilar with the basic principles reflected in the ASEAN Concord II or with subsequent proposals on regional security put forward by Indonesia and some other ASEAN countries.

As a result of these positive developments, Russian-ASEAN political relationship has reached an unprecedented level from being politically correct but sometimes dangerously strained during the Cold War, to the professed common stand on a wide range of important political and security issues. Paradoxically enough however, in spite of these welcome changes, Russia finds itself at present largely on the periphery of national interests and concerns of most ASEAN member-states with the probable exception of Vietnam. Moreover, compared to the Cold War period when Russia (or to be more precise — the Soviet Union) was regarded as an influential strategic actor in Southeast Asia and served as a balancing force in regional politics mostly because of its massive political and military support to its friends and allies here, nowadays Russia's political role in the region became almost directly proportional to the volume of its trade and economic relations with the Southeast Asian states which, in most cases, remains rather low.

In 2004, according to preliminary estimates, the total volume of Russia-ASEAN trade stood below US$4 billion compared to Russia's trade with Japan reaching US$8 billion the same year and Russia's trade with China at around US$20 billion. The largest trading partners of Russia in Southeast Asia were Singapore, Malaysia and Vietnam (in that order) who accounted for over 70 per cent of all Russia's trade turnover with all ASEAN member-states. The bulk of Russia's export to its Southeast Asian trading partners constituted — with a few exceptions like MIG aircraft sales to Malaysia or export of oil and energy equipment to Vietnam — mainly metals and metal products (60 to 80 per cent of its total value) as well as fertilizers and chemical products. Russia's imports consisted mainly of agricultural raw materials and foodstuffs (palm oil, coffee, rice, sugar, fruits, etc.), household electronics and computer software.

Clearly, neither the volume of this trade, nor its structure could be regarded as even remotely satisfactory and reflecting the true economic potentials of Russia and its counterparts in the region. True, certain steps are being contemplated both in Russia and in some ASEAN countries to improve this situation but they are still mostly in the exploratory stage. Russia faces an uphill task of restoring its role in regional politics, including regional security, not only by observing such principles of relationship with these states as pragmatism, equality, mutual respect and non-interference in their domestic affairs, or by making joint political declarations with them, but above all by expanding its economic cooperation with the local countries. When and if Russia is able to solve this problem, it may help to increase its political weight in Southeast Asia.

The basis for facilitating economic ties between Russia and ASEAN has been strengthened lately by the improved economic situation both in Russia and in most of the ASEAN member-states, even in spite of the terrible material and human losses inflicted upon them — Indonesia in particular — by the recent tsunami tragedy.

One of the biggest, if not the biggest, problems in Russia-ASEAN relations, in my opinion, is a gross information gap existing between our societies. Neither the Russian business community, nor the business community in the ASEAN countries are sufficiently informed about each other's market opportunities. There is a glaring absence of regular ASEAN trade fairs in Russia or of similar Russian trade fairs in ASEAN countries. Our governments should liberalize on a mutual basis the existing visa regimes which, in many ASEAN countries as well as in Russia, are too stringent. By doing this they would help to promote tourism in both directions and to create better climate for business visits and cultural exchanges.

Russia is a modern industrial nation with a well-established basis in such areas as space and nuclear technologies, power generation or biochemistry. Responding to the interest existing in the ASEAN member-states to Russian advanced technologies and know-how, Russian companies should be prepared not merely to sell such technologies but to establish joint ventures with local businesses for their use.

Another area of cooperation between Russia and ASEAN that could and should become more intensive is in education and cultural exchanges. Russia may increase substantially the number of students from ASEAN countries in Russian universities and even grant some of them state scholarships. On its part, Russian students may come on a reciprocal basis to study in the universities of Singapore, Thailand, Malaysia, and other ASEAN countries.

I would like to underscore the importance of contacts, like the one we are having today at this seminar, between respective academic communities of Russia and ASEAN. Such contacts, especially if they are regular, may help to achieve better understanding of each other's positions, motivations and concerns regarding a wide range of bilateral, regional and global political, economic and security issues that present serious interest for our respective countries and their governments. In the past there were rather intensive regular contacts of this kind between representatives of our academic communities. But since the middle of the 1990s, they actually stopped — not only for financial reasons but also, probably, for the lack of mutual interest. The situation is changing for the better now, and I am particularly grateful to the ISEAS and its Director, Mr. Kesavapany, who demonstrated profound understanding of the need to restart such contacts by organizing this seminar. I congratulate Mr. Kesavapany and his colleagues in the ISEAS on that remarkable achievement and I hope that next year we shall have another seminar of this kind, this time hosted by my institute, IMEMO, in Moscow.

I would like to complete my short presentation by quoting from the address of President Vladimir Putin sent to the participants of the Tenth ASEAN Summit (Vientiane, November 2004):

> Russia considers ASEAN to be an important and highly influential organization actively contributing to the integration of the Asia-Pacific region. We hold in high esteem the constructive and creative role which ASEAN plays in promoting stability in South East Asia, its economic and social development. Multilateral and multidimensional cooperation with the ASEAN member-states present an important direction of Russia's foreign policy. And we have firm intention to continue building up and strengthening partnership with ASEAN in the interests of peace, stability and progress of our common Asia-Pacific region.

PART II
Bilateral Relations

3

Malaysia and Russia: Strengthening Strategic Partnership in the 21st Century: A Malaysian Perspective

K. S. Nathan

INTRODUCTION: THE TRANSFORMED RELATIONSHIP IN A POST-COLD WAR ENVIRONMENT

For bilateral Malaysia-Russia relations, the decade of the 1990s and beyond has been fundamentally different from the previous era in the light of significant global and regional developments that have occurred since the collapse of the Soviet Union and Empire, and the end of the East-West ideological struggle by 1991. Since then Russia has been transforming its Soviet-era political, economic and military structures to reflect the creation of political democracy and a market economy. The current Russian president, Vladimir Putin, has, since assuming office in 2000, pursued the goal of rapprochement with the West and active participation in the political, economic and security affairs of the Asia-Pacific region including building strong linkages individually and collectively with the ten-member Association of Southeast Asian Nations (ASEAN).

For its part, Malaysia had made rapid strides in industrialization and economic expansion under the visionary leadership of its fourth prime minister, Dr Mahathir Mohamad who held office from 1981–2003. The ASEAN Regional Forum (ARF) became a focal point of activity in regional security matters since its inception in 1993, serving as a critical venue for security dialogues and cooperation to fill the vacuum created by the demise of Cold War power relations. The end of the ideological battle was also marked by the birth of a plethora of new states that were largely constituent elements of the Soviet/Communist empire. Both Malaysia and Russia intend to be active partners in restructuring the regional and world order that has emerged out of the ashes of the Cold War. The Malaysia-Russia relationship is therefore a function of these dramatic developments, as all relationships between nations at the bilateral, regional, or multilateral level are intrinsically connected to systemic change in international relations. It is here that the energies of a dynamically developing Malaysia and a radically transformed Russia could be profitably engaged to give effect and substance to the unfolding new spectrum of bilateral relations.

This chapter addresses the following issues in the context of the prospects for bilateral Malaysia-Russia relations: (a) International Security, (b) Economic Relations, (c) Political and Economic Cooperation: Challenges and Prospects, and Conclusion: Prospects for Bilateral Cooperation in the Post-9/11 Era.

MALAYSIA-RUSSIA RELATIONS AND INTERNATIONAL SECURITY

The 1990s in the Asia-Pacific region were marked by the waning of ideology and the preponderance of economics as the beacon of international security and development. This primary trend in turn spawned parallel and subsidiary processes, convergent as well as divergent, stabilizing as well as destabilizing trends, in an attempt to fill the military vacuum created by the demise of the Cold War: Single Europe marked by the creation of the European Union in 1992, NAFTA (North America Free Trade Area), the development of the Asia-Pacific Economic Cooperation (APEC), the Mahathir-initiated East Asia Economic Grouping (EAEG) initially, and later as a more informal grouping known as East Asia Economic Caucus (EAEC), which now seems to have taken a life of its own under the rubrics of ASEAN+3, East Asian Summit, growth triangles in East and Southeast Asia, and the Asian financial crisis of 1997–98 — all of which produced difficulties as well as opportunities for Malaysia-Russia bilateral cooperation. To be sure, Russian intentions to participate in the economic dynamism of the Asia-Pacific region, and thereby transform the "character" and "content" of Russian foreign policy are to be found in Soviet President Mikhail Gorbachev's doctrinal pronouncements at Vladivostok in July 1986, and Krasnoyarsk in September 1988.

Malaysia-Russia security objectives and concerns converge in the following areas:

(1) Promote nuclear disarmament at the strategic and global level, as this would reduce militaristic tendencies and priorities thereby enhancing the prospects for security based on economic and social development.

(2) Promote regional disarmament *via* the creation of nuclear weapons-free zones (NWFZ), for example in Southeast Asia in the context of ZOPFAN (Zone of Peace, Freedom, and Neutrality). Indeed, this convergence of strategic perspective must be read in the context of a transformed Russia that is no longer a superpower, and a Malaysian desire to assert greater control over its regional security environment with a view to limiting as far as possible, external intervention in regional affairs.

(3) Reduction of the risk of war, the prevention of the militarization of space, the prohibition and destruction of weapons of mass destruction (WMD), and ensuring the security of sea lanes of communication (SLOCs).[1]

(4) The strengthening of ASEAN as a regional forum for political and economic cooperation, and the ASEAN Regional Forum as a vehicle to promote confidence building, preventive diplomacy, and conflict resolution in Asia.

(5) Support for the integrity and sovereignty of the United Nations as the sole arbiter of international conflicts, and as a multilateral forum through which issues of war and peace are settled. In this sense, both are opposed to American unilateralism in shaping regional and world order as it is devoid of universal consensus and participation. President Putin himself cautioned that "if unilateralism becomes the norm, it will lead to chaos and catastrophe".[2] Malaysia would prefer a more active role for the United Nations in the management of international security. The UN mechanism offers the best guarantee for long-term peace and security in a depolarized world. Unipolarity, bipolarity, tripolarity, or any other sectarian security schemes are at best, ineffective substitutes for a UN-managed multipolar world order in which the security of one is the security of all.[3]

Malaysia and Russia view the ARF mechanism as the most acceptable and least controversial lowest common denominator to manage pan-Asian security in the post-Cold War era. The principal features of the ARF may be stated as follows:

(1) It is a security dialogue inviting and engaging all interested and involved participants to express and moderate their security concerns;
(2) It includes all the key Asian and Pacific actors: China, India, Russia, United States, Japan, Korea, and ASEAN;
(3) It is a process involving some informal procedures by which security issues are raised and discussed at the annual meeting;
(4) It is a non-threatening mechanism or security framework as the agenda for discussion is set by ASEAN — a regional grouping whose credibility and political acceptability is beyond question;
(5) It is a confidence-building-measure (CBM) in the sense that the security dialogue rests firmly on a foundation of economic and political consultations *via* the ASEAN-PMC (Post-Ministerial Conference), and builds on this foundation of promise and performance.

The ARF is thus a loose structure of major and minor powers brought together by strategic circumstances that were unpredictable but which require concert to reduce uncertainties arising from major ideological, political, economic, and territorial changes accompanying a major imperial collapse and the demise of Cold War confrontations. The ARF espouses all the fundamental principles of ASEAN's Treaty of Amity and Cooperation (TAC) signed at its first summit in Bali in 1976. Russia acceded to TAC at ASEAN's Vientiane Summit in November 2004, joining other earlier signatories: India, China, Japan, Pakistan, and South Korea. Article 2 of TAC outlines the basic framework for ASEAN security cooperation:

(a) Mutual respect for the independence, sovereignty, equality, territorial integrity and national identity of all nations;
(b) The right of every state to lead its national existence free from external interference, subversion, or coercion;
(c) Non-interference in the internal affairs of one another;
(d) Settlement of differences or disputes by peaceful means;
(e) Renunciation of the threat or use of force; and
(f) Effective cooperation among themselves.

However, Malaysia has misgivings *vis-a-vis* each power. In the case of the United States, the prevailing Pax Americana means unrestrained power wielded by Washington to the detriment of developing nations whose strategic priorities differ from Washington's agenda. In the case of Russia, Malaysia is keenly aware of the internal preoccupation of the Russian leadership with political and economic consolidation under a radically altered politico-ideological framework. Today, Russia is still a very weak actor in world politics. In the case of China, while its rise is welcome and portends many economic opportunities, there is also present the real danger of the Chinese bubble bursting, and creating in its wake economic misery and insecurity for millions who may be forced out as "boat people" onto neighbouring shores. Political and/or economic instability in China is bound to affect the stability of China's East Asian neighbours, including the ASEAN states.

More recently, China's National People's Congress has passed a law legitimizing the use of force to integrate Taiwan should the leadership in Taipei declare independence. While Malaysia is committed to the "One China" policy, it would be wary of a rising China that is boosting its military power for aggressive purposes such as deployment in the contested South China Sea to assert Beijing's sovereignty. Malaysia, along with other ASEAN states — Vietnam, Philippines and Brunei — has overlapping territorial claims in an area that is also claimed by China. Any military assertion by China in the near future could well drive Malaysia and other ASEAN members into a closer alliance with other regional and external powers — United States, India, Japan and Russia — to maintain a balance of power in the Asia-Pacific region.

Malaysia and Russia can enhance prospects for regional and global security by undertaking individually, and collectively, the following measures:

(1) Initiate the process of restructuring the UN Security Council to reflect the phenomenal changes that have taken place over the past eighty-five years (if we calculate from the time the League of Nations (LON) was set up, because the UN borrows the Big Five concept from the LON). The present Security Council structure supports the *status quo* of the Big Five, but certainly does not address the aspirations of new and emerging powers, as well as bourgeoning politico-economic entities that may have much to contribute to international security and development. In sum, Malaysia and Russia could profitably strengthen bilateral cooperation in the political sphere by addressing, perhaps designing, the future of the UN system.

(2) A related step is to enhance cooperation within the framework of the Non-Aligned Movement (NAM). The concept of non-alignment has become irrelevant in an ideological sense, but the structure, principles,

and foundation of non-alignment encompassing most of the world's nation-states (115 out of today's 194) could be applied to promote genuine neutralization, disarmament, and development.

(3) The third and most important area is nuclear disarmament. The challenges posed to regional and world security of a nuclearized North Korea and Iran require stronger international collaboration, and countries which have influence in the Islamic World such as Malaysia, and over North Korea such as Russia (although limited compared to the Soviet era), can play a more active role in curbing nuclear proliferation. Malaysia's strong advocacy of Southeast Asia as a Nuclear Weapons-Free Zone (SEA-NWFZ) signals a firm commitment to nuclear disarmament.

BILATERAL RELATIONS: PROSPECTS FOR ECONOMIC COOPERATION

The historical record of Malaysia-Russia economic relations is dismal. In 1969 (two years after Malaysia established diplomatic relations with the USSR (now Russia)), bilateral trade accounted for only 2.7 per cent of Malaysia's total external trade. In 1979, the figure was 1.2 per cent, and in 1989, that is, after twenty-two years of official relations, the figure stood at 1.3 per cent of Malaysia's external trade, with the trade balance always in Malaysia's favour. Exports in 1989 to Russia accounted for 1.1 per cent of total exports, while imports from Russia represented only 0.5 per cent of total Malaysian imports.[4]

In the past, the crucial factor inhibiting closer economic ties has been the difference in economic ideology and social systems. Today, that gap has been considerably narrowed by the ideological, political and economic transformation of post-Soviet Russia in the past fifteen years, that is, from a command economy to a market economy. In this new Russia, prospects for bilateral economic cooperation have considerably widened, although concrete measures for Malaysian investment, assistance, joint ventures, etc. are yet to be implemented in full. As Russia regularizes processes and procedures towards a full-fledged market economy, the scope for substantive economic interaction is bound to increase over the long term. The generally low volume of bilateral trade, hovering around one percent in the total external trade of both countries for the past thirty years, is expected to improve as both partners attempt to diversify their sources and markets in their overall trade orientation. For instance, Russia's share of Malaysia's total external trade in 1979 was 1.2 per cent, while in 2003 the figure declined to 0.5 per cent. Total trade between Malaysia and Russia in 2003 was US$425 million, an increase of 9.4 per cent over the previous year.[5]

POLITICAL AND ECONOMIC RELATIONS:
CHALLENGES AND PROSPECTS

Bilateral trade, political and economic relations received a boost with the visit of President Putin to Malaysia on 4–5 August 2003. New areas of bilateral cooperation that have been identified are in the following fields: Defence, aerospace, economy, education, and combating terrorism. The Russian leader also signed a US$900 million contract for Malaysian purchases of 18 Sukhoi warplanes (with delivery beginning in 2006) to beef up Malaysia's defence and military capability in line with the country's force modernization policy. Russia was prepared to accept 40 per cent of the payment in Malaysian goods especially palm oil.[6] Bilateral trade totalled US$350 million (RM1.34 billion) in 2002 and reached US$425 million in 2003.[7] For Malaysia, this figure represented a dismal figure of only 0.24 per cent of its total trade value, while for Russia, it accounted for 0.29 per cent of global trade. Another important aspect of cooperation is in training and sending Malaysian astronauts into space — reflecting Malaysian aspirations under Mahathir's Vision 2020.[8]

Concrete steps toward greater economic cooperation might well include the following: Malaysia can take advantage of investment prospects in Russia in terms of (a) setting up banks and finance companies, (b) building hotels, and providing hotel management services, (c) participating in joint ventures for construction of residential accommodation, (d) producing rubber gloves in Russia, (e) increasing substantially exports from the manufacturing sector which now (2004) constitutes 78.4 per cent of total exports. The manufacturing sector is the fastest growing sector of the Malaysian economy, hence Malaysian-Russian economic cooperation must factor in this dimension for the near as well as the long term. The export potential for specific items of Malaysian export to Russia include the following items: (a) electrical machinery, (b) electronic components such as semi-conductors, (c) textiles, clothing, and footwear, (d) toys, and sporting goods, (e) luxury items such as jewellery, gold, and silver, and (f) optical and scientific equipment.[9]

Russian participation in Malaysian economic growth and development could focus on areas where the Eurasian power has been traditionally strong: (a) production of rolling stock to facilitate railroad expansion in Malaysia, (b) greater utilization of the Russian merchant marine for sea-based transportation, (c) agriculture and fisheries development, (d) processing of raw materials and semi-finished goods, and (e) electric power generation and machine building. Furthermore, counter-trade and Russian-Malaysian cooperation in nuclear science and technology offer concrete prospects for bilateral cooperation. In this way, Malaysia can diversify its international trade and economic activity by expanding its trade relations with Russia beyond the traditional items of

Malaysian export (rubber, palm oil and tin), and import (steel, metallurgical equipment, chemical substances, tractors, cotton, and fishing vessels).[10] According to MATRADE, one of the main conditions for future growth of exports to Malaysia and its structural improvement is increase in exports of hi-tech products, and development of technical and investment collaboration with Malaysian companies and organizations. The Malaysian market is said to possess relevant potential for equipment and technologies in the following areas: Information technologies, telecommunication, production and use of composition materials, biotechnology, automation of manufacturing processes, and aerospace technologies (especially commercial space exploration).[11]

Russia, as a European and Asia-Pacific nation, expects to participate actively in European economic integration, as well as in Asia-Pacific regional economic processes including ASEAN and East Asian integration. Malaysian-Russian cooperation in support of basically positive regional economic processes could contribute substantially towards shaping the new world order in which conflicting national interests are "minimized", and cooperative programmes are "maximized". Moreover, post-Soviet Russia itself is an experiment in economic regionalism in which opportunities abound for Malaysians to participate in market-oriented development of the Euro-Asian continent.

CONCLUSION: PROSPECTS FOR BILATERAL COOPERATION IN THE POST-9/11 ERA

Pressures for internal economic reform and external economic integration would cumulatively have the effect of viewing Russia as a friendly and benign power — at least in the near term — rather than one that threatens the stability and prosperity of the Asia-Pacific region. Current domestic developments in the Russian Federation would tend to increase the preoccupation of Moscow's leaders with internal political, constitutional, economic, and social reforms. In viewing the prospective role of Russia as a major power with definitive interests in Southeast Asia at the turn of the twenty-first century, Malaysia and ASEAN would be less concerned about a prospective Russian threat to the security of the region. Conversely, ASEAN would stand to benefit politically and economically by integrating Russian power into the Asian balance comprising the other major powers *viz.* China, Japan, India, and the United States. The rise of China and India in Asia creates additional incentives for Malaysian-Russian strategic engagement in the Asia-Pacific region to ensure a stable equilibrium in the decades ahead.

However, in the short-to-medium term, the relevance of Russian power to Southeast Asia would be largely economic in terms of the economic interaction between the Russian Far East and East Asia — that is, it would expand opportunities for market diversification, and strengthen ASEAN's rising industrial and export potential over the next three decades. The notable shift in Russia's policy towards Asia since 1992 has been Moscow's emphasis on political, trade, and security relations with the former Soviet republics of Central Asia which contains an ethnic Russian population of over 9.5 million. This new political, economic, and security orientation has led to "a steady expansion of Russian influence in the new states of Central Asia, and in one case (Tajikistan) — military intervention".[12] With respect to Southeast Asia, Russian interest would increasingly focus on economic cooperation with ASEAN as a strategy to influence the regional balance of power in favour of Moscow's long-term political and security interests *vis-a-vis* China, Japan, the United States and India.

The strategic environment confronting Russia in the first decade of the twenty-first century — both in its internal and external dimensions is complex given the dynamics and dangers of post-Soviet democratization and development. Russia remains a major military and nuclear power, with vast resources for exploitation and development in the Russian Far East. Russia's threat perceptions of China, Japan, Korea, and the United States is a critical factor conditioning Russian foreign policy. Indeed the "Russian Question" is a critical variable in the Asia-Pacific balance of power. A favourable security environment at the global and regional levels would certainly conduce to positive bilateral and multilateral economic cooperation beneficial to Russia and its neighbours in the Asia Pacific. In this regard, Malaysia has signed a military agreement with Russia during Putin's 2003 visit, to purchase sixteen Su-30MKM fighter aircraft worth over US$900 million as part of its policy of diversification of sources of defence weaponry, while representing a further endorsement of its policy of equidistance with major external powers. The new agreement supplements an earlier purchase in the 1990s of 18 MIG 29SE fighters worth US$615 million. Bilateral military cooperation is expected to strengthen if Russian suppliers prove capable of overcoming logistical problems related to post-sale servicing, which Malaysia had to contend with in the 1990s.[13]

Russia's successful engagement with ASEAN and the broader Asia Pacific in the next decade requires concerned efforts by regional players who view Russia's peaceful integration into the security architecture of the Asia Pacific an exercise in mutual benefit. Although it is undeniable that Russia's security role in the Asia-Pacific region including Southeast Asia has declined considerably, Moscow's future role should not be discounted. In the post-9/11 era, both ASEAN and Russia share a common platform in the war against international terrorism as it impacts significantly on internal stability as well as regional and global security. Russia is as much concerned about the security of SLOCs as it emerges as a major trading partner of ASEAN countries which straddle the Straits of Malacca through which passes a significant portion of world trade. In this context, ASEAN and Russia endorsed cooperation in the area of transnational crime by signing the ASEAN-Russia Joint Declaration on Cooperation in Combating International Terrorism at the PMC+1 session in Jakarta (2 July 2004).

In the near term, that is, within five to ten years, Russia can be expected to resurge as a major world power with a capacity to project its security interests in this region. Russia's political, economic, and military involvement in the Asia Pacific contributes to the emergence of a stable Russian foreign policy *vis-a-vis* Central Asia. Russia's isolation could result in an inward focus of Russian security concerns, with additional pressures by Moscow on its former Soviet republics. Moscow's eagerness to join the fifty-seven-member Organization of Islamic Conference (OIC), either as a member or observer, given that it has a Muslim population exceeding twenty million, is indicative of the recognition given by the New Russia to religious freedom and pluralism. Furthermore, in the post-9/11 era, Moscow's policies towards ethno-religious minorities including its handling of the Chechen problem need to be better understood by the world Muslim community. Both Malaysia and Russia are equally committed to fight the war against terror, recognizing at the same time, that terrorism is a manifestation of serious sociopolitical and economic inequalities, and unsettled conflicts in which the protagonists are unable to make the necessary compromises.[14] In this regard, building closer relations with moderate Muslim nations like Malaysia and gaining their support are considered vital elements of Russian foreign policy under President Putin. Russian national security dictates that Russia be viewed and accepted as a positive player in the Asia-Pacific balance of power, and Malaysian-Russian political, economic and security cooperation therefore become integral components in realization of this objective in Southeast Asian regional security. In this regard, the ASEAN-PMC Ten+1 with Russia, held in Vientiane on 28 July 2005, welcomed the strengthening of ASEAN-Russia dialogue relations and the first ever ASEAN-Russia Summit to be held in Malaysia in December 2005. The meeting, held in conjunction with the 11th ASEAN Summit in Kuala Lumpur (12–14 December 2005), is expected to further strengthen bilateral ties between Malaysia and Russia.

NOTES

1. Even as early as 1991, prior to the collapse of the Soviet Union, the principles of post-Soviet Russia's foreign policy were already being articulated by the outgoing Soviet Government. See speech by Igor Rogachev, Deputy Foreign Minister of the USSR, "USSR-ASEAN: A New Level of Relations", *Berita Soviet* published by the Information Department, USSR Embassy in Malaysia, no. 3563, 18 July 1991, p. 3.
2. Hardev Kaur, "Russia Eyes Asian Economies". Interview with President Putin at Novo Ogoryovo, his official residence outside Moscow, prior to his visit to Malaysia on 4–5 August 2003. *New Straits Times*, 8 July 2003.
3. Mahathir Mohamad, Prime Minister of Malaysia, "Let's Strive for a Freer UN". Speech at the 46th UN General Assembly on 24 September 1991. Excerpts published in *New Straits Times*, 27 September 1991, p. 8.
4. *Direction of Trade Statistics Yearbook 1990*, Washington, D.C.: International Monetary Fund, 1990, p. 266.
5. MATRADE (Malaysia External Trade Development Corporation): <http://www.matrade.gov.my/market-info/country-profiles/cp-russia2.htm>, p. 2.
6. <http://english.pravda.ru/main/18/89/357/10668_su.html>.
7. MATRADE(Malaysia External Trade Development Corporation): <http://www.matrade.gov.my/market-info/country-profiles/cp-russia2.htm>, p. 2.
8. "Malaysia to Launch Program in 2005 to Send Astronaut to Space". Special Press Summary: "Putin's Trip to Malaysia, 4–5 August 2003", p. 12: <http://www.vic-info.org/RegionsTop.nsf/0/dddb20aa416f2ba80a256d7c000c5592/$FILE/030806-SPS-Putin'sTriptoMalaysia-web.doc>.
9. MATRADE(Malaysia External Trade Development Corporation): <http://www.matrade.gov.my/market-info/country-profiles/cp-russia2.htm>, pp. 2–5.
10. K.S. Nathan, "Malaysia and the Soviet Union: A Relationship with a Distance", *Asian Survey* 27, no. 10 (October 1987): 1072.
11. MATRADE (Malaysia External Trade Development Corporation): <http://www.matrade.gov.my/market-info/country-profiles/cp-russia2.htm>, p. 5.
12. Herbert J. Ellison and Bruce A. Acker, *The New Russia and Asia: 1991–1995*, Seattle, USA: The National Bureau of Asian Research, 1996, pp. 7–8.
13. "Russia and Malaysia to Sign Large Arms Deal". Special Press Summary: "Putin's Trip to Malaysia, 4–5 August 2003", p. 8: <http://www.vic-info.org/RegionsTop.nsf/0/dddb20aa416f2ba80a256d7c000c5592/$FILE/030806-SPS-Putin'sTriptoMalaysia-web.doc>.
14. "Russia Eyes Asian Economies", *New Straits Times*, 8 July 2003.

4
Indonesia-Russia Relations: The Jakarta Perspective

Leo Suryadinata

Indonesia-Russia relations started since the end of World War II and early relations were poor but became close during the Sukarno period due to Jakarta's anti-colonial stand. Nevertheless, the relations began to cool after the fall of Sukarno. They further declined during the Suharto era and continued to be cold during the post-Soviet period, following the end of the Cold War. This chapter deals briefly with Indonesia-Russia relations from early post-World War II until now, mainly from the Indonesian perspective. It looks at the nature of their relationships and major factors which influence Indonesian relations with the Soviet Union/Russian Federation. The ideological and economic aspects are examined, so are prospects of the relations.

There have been a few studies on Indonesia-Soviet relations during the Cold War as the ideological struggle was important. Nevertheless, since the end of the Cold War and the disintegration of the Soviet Union in 1991, studies on Jakarta-Moscow relations have been markedly reduced. This is understandable as the Russian power has declined and the focus of world politics has shifted from ideology to economics. The economic relations between Indonesia and Russia were minimal. It is worth noting that even the Indonesian Central Board of Statistics no longer recorded the trade value between Jakarta and Moscow from 1999 onwards, showing the insignificance of the Indonesian-Russian trade. I will return to this point later in the chapter.

EARLY RELATIONS: FROM ANIMOSITY TO COOPERATION

Indonesia-Soviet relations, like relations between Indonesia and the United States of America, date back to the revolutionary period when Indonesia was still trying to defend its independence. The Soviets supported the communist group in order to gain more influence in the newly independent Indonesia. However, during the communist rebellions in 1948 known as the Madiun Affair, the pro-Soviet communists were crushed. This marked the decline of Indonesia-Soviet relations for the next ten years. Relations improved again when there was a resurgence of Indonesian nationalism and rebirth of the left-wing movement. This coincided with the campaign to liberate West Irian (now Papua) where the West refused to assist the Sukarno government. Jakarta then turned to both the Soviets and the People's Republic of China (PRC) for help. Soviet military assistance was most significant, and this helped to bring the two countries closer.

Moscow's relations with the Indonesian Communist Party (PKI) during the Sukarno era were not cordial. There were two groups within the PKI: A pro-Moscow group allegedly led by Njoto and the dominant Aidit group, which was oriented towards Beijing. Nevertheless, there was no open split within the party. After the 1965 coup, because of the pro-Beijing elements in the party, Moscow was quite critical of PKI leadership. It accused the PKI of having abandoned Marxist-Leninist teachings and adopting Mao Zedong Thought.[1] It also criticized the PKI for not preventing extremist officers from staging a military coup leading to "a reign of terror against the Communist Party and other democratic organizations".[2] Moscow, in fact, noted that the army had been responsible for the coup and that the coup was not initiated by the PKI. Ironically, it also said that the PKI might have been able to "curb the extremist feelings of a group of officers",[3] indicating that the PKI had control or influence over the group.

THE SUHARTO PERIOD: RELATIONS COOL DOWN

After the 1965 coup, the Soviets "denounced the persecution of democrats and communists".[4] Moscow harboured some PKI leaders and left-wing Indonesians. In spite of this, Jakarta-Moscow relations were not suspended, mainly due to the insignificant role played by the Soviets in the coup. Nevertheless, the immediate post-coup period saw a deterioration of Indonesia-

Soviet relations. In 1968, Soviet leaders requested that the Indonesian Government spare the life of three PKI leaders involved in the coup, but the request was refused.[5] Despite Jakarta's anti-communist attitude, the Soviets were still eager to improve relations with Indonesia. Jakarta also wanted to maintain relations with Moscow to gain certain economic benefits. Thus, in 1979, Adam Malik visited Moscow to request the rescheduling of Indonesia's debt repayment. An agreement was eventually signed, but trade and economic relations with Moscow did not improve significantly.

At the time when Jakarta began to demand more economic aid, Jakarta-Moscow relations appeared somewhat improved. The two sides signed an agreement on technical and economic cooperation in 1974. With this, Indonesia expected softer loan terms from the Soviets and hoped to project an image that Indonesia was still non-aligned. In 1975 it was announced that the Soviets would build two hydroelectric plants in Indonesia.[6] Nevertheless, economic cooperation was limited because the terms of the agreement were not really soft and the Soviets appeared to have limited resources for helping developing countries. The Indonesians found that they still had to rely heavily on the West and Japan for economic assistance and loans.

After 1969, when the Soviets attempted to form an alliance with some Asian and Southeast Asian states in an "Asian Collective Security System" with the aim of encircling the People's Republic of China (PRC), Indonesia was not interested in joining the club. Although Indonesia had always been critical of the PRC's behaviour, it did not want to get involved in a Sino-Soviet rivalry. Basically, it did not trust the Soviets. This can be seen in the Indonesian armed forces newspaper, *Angkatan Bersenjata*'s response to the Soviet proposal: "We in Indonesia believe that regional cooperation for prosperity is better than a defence system. We think that no Southeast Asian country is eager to join the Soviet defence system. The invitation is unwelcome."[7]

The military in Jakarta was also concerned with the Moscow-New Delhi alliance and its possible impact on the security of the Indian (Indonesian) Ocean.[8] The military noted, however, that as long as the U.S. Seventh Fleet was present, there was no imminent danger. Moreover, the military noted that Moscow was far from Indonesia and, therefore, did not present an immediate threat to the security of Indonesia.[9]

Minor friction occurred in the early 1982 when Indonesia (following Malaysia) expelled two Russian spies from the country.[10] The affair did not jeopardize Indonesia-Soviet relations however. In fact, in the 1980s the Soviets began to court Indonesia again. Many Soviet leaders visited Indonesia. In 1986, for instance, a Soviet delegation led by Salimov Akil Uturzanovich conveyed a message from the Soviet president, Andrei Gromyko, to Suharto inviting him to visit the USSR.[11] Suharto accepted the invitation but did not visit the country until three years later. Apparently, Suharto did not think it necessary to be close to Moscow.

Nevertheless, the Soviets had some supporters within Indonesia. One of them was the *Merdeka* group. It is worth noting that Russian publications often described the Indonesian newspapers, *Merdeka* and the defunct *Sinar Harapan* as nationalistic.[12] It is not by coincidence that Gorbachev gave a special interview to *Merdeka* on his new policy.[13] In addition, many observers maintained that a Soviet bank gave financial assistance to the *Merdeka* group, but this was denied by *Merdeka*.[14] It is not known which particular generals were behind *Merdeka*, but it is generally believed that the newspaper had the support of a segment of the military elite in Indonesia.

LATE-SUHARTO PERIOD: IMPROVED RELATIONS

Since the 1965 coup, President Suharto did not visit Moscow until September 1989 when he went there after attending the Non-Aligned Movement conference in Belgrade.[15] The desire of Indonesia, and especially of President Suharto, to project a higher profile in world affairs and to become chairman of the Non-Aligned Movement, was the major motivation for his visit to Moscow.[16] During the visit, Suharto expressed his thanks for Soviet assistance to Indonesia during the West Irian campaign.[17] He also agreed to foster economic relations.[18] It was reported, however, that Suharto told Gorbachev that Indonesia would not change its stance on communism but stated that his country bore no feelings of enmity towards communist countries.[19]

It is worth noting that Suharto's visit to the Soviet Union began in the Republic of Uzbeck which is well known for its great Islamic heritage.[20] Only after visiting Tashkent and Samarkand, two Islamic holy places, did Suharto and his delegation proceed to Leningrad and Moscow. Suharto's visit to the Muslim republic and the Islamic holy places can be seen as a gesture aimed at Muslims both at home and abroad. It was also intended to gain the support of the Islamic countries in the Non-Aligned Movement (NAM).

The relations between Suharto's Indonesia and Gorbachev's Russia improved significantly. For one thing, Gorbachev's policy had downgraded the importance of ideology and military force and in favour of pragmatism and diplomacy. This was shown by his new policy towards the West, China and Southeast Asia.[21] Courting Indonesia was part of this strategy, and Jakarta responded to this new policy. When there was a coup in August 1991 aimed at overthrowing Gorbachev, Indonesia expressed its concern with the stability of the Union.[22] Suharto himself was quoted as saying that the solution should be in accordance with the "wish of the Soviet people", and it should not have a negative impact on the Soviet Union.[23] Apparently, Suharto was not eager to support the coup launched by communist hardliners. And when Gorbachev made his comeback, Suharto immediately congratulated the Soviet president, indicating that he preferred Gorbachev to the coup leader.[24]

It is interesting to note that Jakarta did not insist that the Soviets suspend ties with the communist parties in Southeast Asia as a condition for better relations. Apparently, in the Indonesian perception, the links between the communist parties of the USSR and the Southeast Asian states did not affect the political stability of the region or, more precisely, did not affect Indonesia's stability. Also, at the beginning of the 1990s, the USSR eventually disintegrated and was replaced by the Commonwealth of Independent States (CIS), of which the Russian Federation has become the dominant state.

THE POST-COLD WAR PERIOD: ECONOMICS TAKES COMMAND

The disintegration of the USSR spelt the end of the Cold War and the demise of the ideological conflict. Communism was no longer a threat to the West; the United States began to shift its attention to the human rights issue. During the Cold War, the United States tolerated the military regime in Indonesia and also the invasion and occupation of East Timor in 1976. However, with the end of the Cold War and change in the international political climate, Washington began to be critical of the New Order's human rights records, especially in East Timor. Since 1996, Washington started to sever military relations with Jakarta, especially the joint training programme. It also announced the arms embargo on Suharto's Indonesia. Without new arms and spare parts, the Indonesian military suffered a setback in its fighting capabilities. The arms embargo and suspension of the joint military training continued after the fall of Suharto.

During the Habibie and Gus Dur presidencies, due to the weak government and presence of internal problems, Indonesia became more inward rather than outward looking. However, when Megawati replaced Gus Dur to become Indonesia's president, she was interested in projecting a high-profile policy and hence attempted to use the former Eastern Bloc to balance the Western Bloc again. The purpose was to show the United States that Jakarta would be able to purchase arms from the non-Western states.

Not surprisingly, Megawati visited Russia in late April 2003, coinciding with the U.S.-led war against Iraq despite the opposition of three other major powers (including Russia) in the UN. Jakarta's view on the matter was similar to Moscow's and this easily brought the two countries together. Megawati's visit to Russia was part of her ten-day East European trip starting on 17 April. It was also linked to Indonesia's effort to look for new weapon supplies, as there was an embargo on arms sales to Indonesia by the United States due to the alleged human rights abuses ten years ago.[25] Indeed, Megawati was able to conclude a number of purchases with Russia, including the Sukhoi aircraft, which later became a topic of debate in the Indonesian parliament. Towards the end of the visit, Megawati stated in Moscow that Jakarta and Moscow would cooperate in the "project of joint production in the military industry".[26]

The purchase of the Sukhoi aircraft was believed to have been done improperly. The Indonesian parliament initiated a motion to impeach President Megawati, but it was unsuccessful. One commentator noted that, "The failure of the scheme to impeach Megawati over the Sukhoi deal also foiled the U.S. connection that had sought to stop the purchase of Russian military equipment and undermine Russia-Indonesia relations, which act as a strategic counterweight to American domination in Southeast Asia."[27]

Nevertheless, an Indonesian diplomat told me that the purchase of weapons from Russia was insignificant as Indonesia did not rely on Russia for weapon supplies; therefore, it is incorrect to argue that Russia was a strategic counterweight. Nevertheless, Megawati wanted to use Russia to pressurize the United States to lift the embargo. Washington did not restore military relations with Indonesia as Megawati was perceived as a "nationalist" and a weak leader. Only after Susilo Bambang Yudhoyono became the president, did Washington begin to approach Jakarta again and military relations have been partially restored.

PROBLEMS IN IMPROVING RELATIONS

Although relations between Jakarta and Moscow improved somewhat both during the late Suharto period and the Megawati presidency, closer relations were difficult to achieve owing partly to the fact that not much economic benefit could be derived by Indonesia in such relations. Ideology was an issue during the early Suharto era but it has no longer been since the late Suharto period and beyond. The economic factor may have been the main reason for the limited improvement in the relations. Examining the trade volume between Indonesia and CIS/Russia in the last four years of the Suharto rule, it is clear that it only constituted a very small portion of the Indonesian overseas trade. Comparing the trade between Indonesia and Japan or between Indonesia and the United States, the proportion of Indonesia-CIS/Russia trade was insignificant (see Tables 1, 2 and 3 in Appendix 1). In 1994, for instance,

Indonesia-CIS/Russia trade value was only US$310 million; it was 1.6 per cent of the Indonesia-Japan trade and 3.2 per cent of the Indonesia-U.S. trade.[28] In fact, trade between Jakarta and Moscow continued to decline over the period 1998–2003. In 2003, for instance, the Indonesia-Russia trade value only achieved US$210 million or 1.8 per cent of the Indonesia-Japan trade and 2.1 per cent of the Indonesia-U.S. trade.[29] Not surprisingly, in the Indonesian Statistical Year Book published by the Central Board of Statistics (BPS) in Jakarta, there are no published records regarding Indonesia's trade with the CIS/Russia, because the trade value between these two countries has been too insignificant to be listed separately. Politically, it had no significant impact on Indonesia. This also explains why there was no major study on Indonesia's post-Cold War relations with Russia.

CONCLUDING REMARKS

Economic factors have been most important in Indonesia's relations with the major powers since the New Order. Relations with the United States and Japan have been close as a result of Indonesia's economic dependence on them. On the other hand, the lack of close relations between Jakarta and Moscow can partly be explained in terms of the absence of significant economic ties. It should be noted, however, that during the Cold War era, the different political ideology of Jakarta and Moscow contributed to the lukewarm relations between the two countries but the disintegration of the Soviet Union in December 1991 made the ideological issue irrelevant.

Suharto and the military were heavily involved in making Indonesia's policy towards major powers. On many occasions, Suharto himself went out of his way to obtain aid and loans for Indonesia. Suharto and the military were instrumental in Indonesia's relations with the now defunct Soviet Union. An improvement in relations coincided with Sino-Soviet rapprochement and Suharto's desire for Indonesia to play a major role in the international arena.

After the fall of Suharto, Jakarta-Moscow relations improved somewhat but due to Russia's limited economic capability after the disintegration of the USSR, the relations have not been as close as with two other big powers, namely the United States and Japan. However, since Indonesia has continued to pursue a free and independent foreign policy, it has not given up the idea of balancing big powers in Southeast Asia. In this context, Russia has been perceived in Jakarta as a potential power, which could balance the presence of the United States and Japan. Nevertheless, in reality because of Russia's decline after the demise of the USSR, it is unlikely that Russia would be able to play that role. Russia's current limited economic capability also serves as a hindrance for closer Jakarta-Moscow ties.

Appendix 1

Table 1
Import (US$ million)

Country	1994	1995	1996	1997	1998	1999	2000	2001	2002	2003
Japan	7,740	9,218	8,504	8,252	4,292	2,913	5397	4,589	4,409	4,228
USA	3,587	4,755	5,059	5,440	3,517	2,841	3,393	3,210	2,644	2,702
Russia	220	438	378	287	30	50	110	141	151	100

Source: *Statistik Indonesia 1998*, p. 344 (for 1994–98); IMF: *Direction of Trade Statistics, Year 2004*, pp. 250–51 (for 1999–2003).

Table 2
Export (US$ million)

Country	1994	1995	1996	1997	1998	1999	2000	2001	2002	2003
Japan	10,929	12,288	12,885	12,485	9,116	10,391	14,415	13,010	12,045	13,603
USA	5,828	6,321	6,794	7,148	7,031	6,908	8,489	7,761	7,570	7,386
Russia	90	134	134	86	39	34	57	62	66	110

Source: *Statistik Indonesia 1998*, p. 321 (for 1994–98); IMF: *Direction of Trade Statistics, Year 2004*, pp. 250–51 (for 1999–2003).

Table 3
Import and Export (US$ million)

Country	1994	1995	1996	1997	1998	1999	2000	2001	2002	2003
Japan	18,669	21,506	21,389	20,737	13,408	13,310	19,812	17,699	16,454	17,831
USA	9,415	11,076	11,853	12,588	10,548	9,749	11,882	10,971	10,214	10,088
Russia	310	572	512	373	69	84	167	203	217	210

Source: *Statistik Indonesia 1998*, pp. 321 and 344 (for 1994–1998); IMF: *Direction of Trade Statistics, Year 2004*, pp. 250–51 (for 1999–2003).

NOTES

* Part of this chapter is based on his earlier book entitled *Indonesia's Foreign Policy Under Suharto: Aspiring to International Leadership*. Singapore: Times Academic Press, 1996, pp. 138–57.

1. V.I. Popov et al., eds. *A Study of Soviet Foreign Policy* (translated by David Skvirsky), Moscow: Progress Publishers, 1975, p. 111.
2. Ibid, p. 112.
3. Ibid.
4. Ibid.
5. K.S. Nathan, *Detente and Soviet Policy in Southeast Asia*, Kuala Lumpur: Gateway Publishing House, 1984, p. 108.
6. Robert C. Horn, "The Soviet Union and Asian Security", *Changing Patterns of Security and Stability in Asia*, edited by Sudershan Chawla and D.R. Sardesai. New York: Praeger, 1980, p. 81.
7. *Angkatan Bersenjata's* editorial. Cited in Helmut G. Callis, "The Role of Indonesia in Asian Regionalism", paper prepared for the Fifth Annual Conference of ASPAC, June 24–27, 1970, p. 19.
8. Sajidiman Surjohadiprodjo, *Langkah-langkah Perdjoangan Kita*, Jakarta: Departemen Pertahanan Keamanan Pusat Sedjarah ABRI, 1971, p. 159.
9. It should be noted that in recent years, Jakarta began to be concerned with Indian naval activities. For instance, Indonesia was disturbed by the report that India was planning to build a major naval based on Great Nicobar Island. See FEER, 15 May 1986. The Indonesian military at one time protested against the "expansion" of the Indian navy, but the Indian authority insisted that it carried out only normal activities. See Mohamed Ayoob, *India and Southeast Asia: Indian Perceptions and Policies*. London and New York: Routledge, 1991, pp. 42–45.
10. For this episode, see H. Rosihan Anwar, *Indonesia 1966–1983: Dari Koresponden Kami di Jakarta*. Jakarta: Grafitipers, 1992, p. 239. It was reported that the Soviets were obtaining sea charts, "probably for their submarine operations". The persons involved were a Soviet embassy official, the Jakarta manager of Aeroflot and an Indonesian naval officer. *Asia Year Book 1983 (FEER)*, p. 162.
11. *Jakarta Post*, 2 June 1986.
12. *Merdeka's* views have often been quoted by Moscow's and Hanoi's publications as representing Indonesia. See for instance, "Beijing Expansionist Plans in Southeast Asia", *International Affairs* (Moscow), no. 6 (1979), pp. 22–23; Hoang Nguyen, "When the Hoa Becomes Beijing Political Cards Against Vietnam", *The Hoa in Vietnam, Dossier II* (Hanoi, 1978), p. 16. It is also noticeable that in the last decade, the Merdeka Group published numerous articles attacking the PRC and the West. For instance, *Merdeka's* Editorial "Strategi Neo-Kolonial", 18 January 1980, and a book entitled *Ancaman Dari Utara* (Jakarta, 1980). The

latest example was its editorial on 25 February 1989 in which it stated that the PRC could not be trusted as China has stabbed Indonesia in the back since the era of Kublai Khan. Note that *Sinar Harapan* was banned and *Suara Pembaruan* was permitted to publish in its place. After Suharto stepped down, *Sinar Harapan* was revived, co-existing with *Suara Pembaruan*.

13. For the text of the interview, see *Soviet News* (Soviet embassy, Singapore), 30 July 1987, p. 3; Also "Answers by M.S. Gorbachev to the Questions of the Indonesian Newspapers Merdeka", in *Press Release* (USSR Singapore embassy), no. 37/87, pp. 1–5.

14. Rodney Tasker in his article entitled "Stopping Any Shade of Red" stated that: "Three years ago the paper [*Merdeka*] is understood to have received a US$3.5 million loan from the Soviets" (*FEER*, 24 August 1979, p. 24). Nurman Diah (son of B.M. Diah) denied this. He wrote that "*Merdeka* had no need of any loan, either from the West or from the Soviets." But Diah noted in the same letter that "The latest expansion of *Merdeka* was in 1971, when it modernized its plant with some modern presses. A foreign bank gave the loan, now repaid to the last cent." There was no mention of the bank's name. "Letters to the Editor: Asia and the Power of the Soviets", *FEER*, 19 October 1979, p. 8.

15. "Era Baru Itu Sudah Dimulai", *Tempo*, 16 September 1989, pp. 14–16.

16. Alatas insisted that the visit was primarily to discuss the promotion of economic contact. *Tempo*, 16 September 1989, p.16. However, Juwono Sudarsono in his article in *Tempo* noted that "there is a strong belief that the visit may convince the leaders in Asia, Africa and Latin America, particularly the first and the second generation leaders who still possess the characteristics of 'revolutionaries' that Indonesia ... would not want to side with either the U.S. camp or the Soviet camp." See "Indonesia dan Uni Soviet", *Tempo*, 16 September 1989, p. 22. Apparently, it is related to Jakarta's desire to be accepted as the leader of the Non-Aligned Movement.

17. *Jakarta Post*, 9 September 1989.

18. The Soviet-Indonesian trade was small but was in Indonesia's favour. In 1986 Indonesian exports to the Soviets amounted to US$51.99 million, but Indonesian imports from the Soviets were only US$5.25 million. In 1987, Indonesian exports to the Soviets increased to US$82.40 million while Indonesian imports from the Soviets were US$15.46 million. Indonesia exported to the Soviets included rubber, pepper, coffee, palm oil, spices and cloths. Imports included fertilizer, textile machine etc. See "Editorial", *Angkatan Bersenjata*, 12 September 1989.

19. See Soedjati Djiwandono, "Indonesia's Response to Soviet Initiatives: An Update", paper submitted to IV World Congress for Soviet and East European Studies, Harrogate, England, July 21–16, 1990, p. 18; See also *Jakarta Post*, 13 September 1989.

20. *Angkatan Bersenjata*, 12 September 1989, p. 1 and editorial.

21. Graeme Gill, "The Soviet Union and Southeast Asia: A New Beginning?" *Contemporary Southeast Asia* 10, no. 1 (June 1988): 69–81.
22. "Tajuk Rencana", *Angkatan Bersenjata*, 22 August 1991.
23. *Kompas*, 22 August 1991.
24. *Kompas*, 23 August 1991.
25 Bantarto Bandoro, "Significance of Mega's East European Trip", *Jakarta Post*, 2 May 2003.
26 "Indonesia-Rusia Sepakati Kerja Sama Militer" [Indonesia and Russia Agree to have Military Cooperation], *Kompas*, 22 April 2003.
27 Laksamana, ed., "Soewandi, Sukhoi and the U.S. Connection", September 10, 2003, Net: The Politics and Economic Portal, 13 March 2005.
28 Computed from Table 3, See Appendix 1.
29 Computed from Table 3, see Appendix 1.

PART III
Security Issues in Southeast Asia

5
Terrorism in Southeast Asia

Sidney Jones

Ms Sidney Jones, Southeast Director of the International Crisis Group and a Visiting Fellow at ISEAS, discussed security threats in the region, notably Jemaah Islamiyah (JI). She noted that terrorism was not viewed as the biggest threat within the region. It was not regime-threatening, although terrorist organizations such as the JI had some capability for violence. The JI was based in Indonesia. Other groups also had broad connections. As the JI weakened, other groups would rise. In the Philippines, there were the MILF, Abu Sayaf and Balek Islam; such groups were mainly used as foot-soldiers. There was no hard evidence of external connections/JI involvement in the terrorism in Southern Thailand. Local issues were usually the prime drivers behind terrorist attacks. But the persecution of Muslims in Chechnya, as well as in Palestine, Iraq and elsewhere, were always cited as grievances in JI documents. In Afghanistan, the recruits from Southeast Asia had trained separately, by themselves. JI leaders had met Khatab in Afghanistan, and Chenchnya was viewed in "romantic terms" by Indonesian mujaheedin, who always had an article about Chechen resistance in their bulletins. There were also video cassettes circulating in Indonesia with titles such as "Hell in Russia". It was known that three JI members had visited Chechnya. Afghanistan formed the bond between the mujaheedin, and Afghan alumni were the most important core members of "special operations" or suicide bombings. They had carried out the Marriott Hotel attack in Jakarta. From 1984 to 1995, most training had been done in camps in Saada (Pakistan) and Khost and Torkham in Afghanistan, where Indonesians had trained, together with some Filipinos and Tajiks. An academy with a three-year training programme had been set up by the JI in Afghanistan. In 1994, the JI decided to move their training camp to Mindanao. It was in operation from 1996 to 2000. One hundred and seventy-five Indonesians and thirty Malaysians had attended courses there. Small groups went to assist the MILF after 2000. This training continued till this year. The leadership and base of the JI were to be found in Indonesia. Even though about 400 arrests had been made, the JI could fill the vacancies. These arrests had weakened the JI but it had generated the impetus for new kinds of terrorist collaboration. For instance, Southeast Asians had gone to Karachi for study, with the aim of keeping the JI alive outside the region. In 2003, one cell was uncovered in Pakistan. While it contained only about fifteen members, the concern was that others might be recruited from amongst the hundreds of Southeast Asians studying quite legitimately in Pakistan. The younger brother of Hambali was arrested in Karachi; Hambali had himself been sheltered in Thailand. Jones stressed that most governments had focused on law enforcement measures, but this was only part of the picture. The JI leaders had sent their children to study both in JI schools in Indonesia, and in the case of the Karachi group, abroad, so a new generation of terrorists was being trained. So governments need to study recruitment patterns, which could not be easily stopped. There was also a need to pay attention to fake documentation; corruption; leaky border controls; access to small arms and explosives, stolen or bought from certain armies or quarries.

6

Southeast Asian Security Challenges: A View from Russia

Victor Sumsky

THE BURDENS OF STUDYING ASEAN

In a sense, the mere diligent registration of ASEAN-related events and schemes, not to mention academic analysis, has never been such a difficult task as it is now. By the standards of the association's recent past, the number of statements, programmes and plans generated after the outbreak of the Asian crisis is stunning. Summits deemed historical are often separated from each other by just a few months. New political, economic and cultural initiatives — some of subregional character, others of intercontinental scope — are announced while implementation of those produced and publicized before them have barely started. One way to realize the magnitude of this process is to look at the list of official ASEAN acronyms on the association's website. Consisting of fourteen pages in small font, it contains, along with catchy, comprehensible and easy-to-pronounce formulas like VAP (Vientiane Action Programme), not a few clumsy abbreviations (for instance, FOCPF standing for the Future Oriented Cooperation Projects Fund) plus such pearls of bureaucratic creativity as IDEA (The Initiative for the Development of East Asia) and ACCORD (ASEAN-China Cooperative Operations in Response to Dangerous Drugs).[1] What is this — a sign of vibrancy or a reflection of vulnerability in a quickly changing world? One unfortunate

historical parallel that comes to mind is Sukarno's Guided Democracy — an
era when a seemingly powerful regime was inventing acronyms by the dozen
trying to dress reality up to its tastes and slipping in the meantime into a
deadly crisis.

WHAT'S NEW ABOUT THE NEW SECURITY THREATS?

Be it as it may, it must be acknowledged that some issues arousing concern
in the ASEAN capitals are called in the association's documents by their
names. These are terrorism, sea piracy, human smuggling, drug trafficking
and new diseases, known together in the official parlance as the New Security
Threats. Obviously, all and each of them represent a serious problem. But are
they so terribly new? For instance, is drug-trafficking so novel to Southeast
Asia? To find an answer, just think about what the name of Golden Triangle
stands for. As for sea piracy, Spanish Manila was less than five years old when
a legendary Chinese corsair Limahong nearly destroyed it. And anyone
seeking information on new diseases should go back to the experience of
those GIs who were bringing home exotic venereal infections from Indochina
wars. Thus, the New Security Threats are not so new in themselves. What is
really new here is the post-Cold War transnational environment in which
occurrences once considered purely local display a capacity to acquire regional
and global meanings in a wink of an eye. Isn't it worthwhile, therefore, to pay
more attention than officials would normally pay to the impact of that
environment on ASEAN, its self-perceptions and prospects?

THE ASEAN MODEL OF MODERNIZATION AND ITS FATE

Summarizing the present state of regional affairs, an outside observer may
conclude that some Southeast Asian economies have recovered from the
shock of the Asian crisis, but ASEAN as a political entity has not. Why? An
often mentioned reason is the heavy damage suffered by Indonesia — until
the fall of Suharto the undisputed political leader of the group. Latent
tensions between several member states have also been sharpened in the heat
of the crisis. On top of that, the latter broke out precisely at the moment of
ASEAN's enlargement, making it more difficult than ever to give multilateral
responses to internal and external trials. Along with these well-known factors
at least one more, not often talked about, might be mentioned: Among the
crisis victims — and, in a wider sense, the victims of globalization — is
nothing less than the ASEAN model of modernization (or AMM for short —
the author's humble addition to the panoply of ASEAN's acronyms). As
something shared by the original ASEAN five and helping to boost their

growth during the Cold War years, AMM may be reduced to the following three features: First, a rightist authoritarian regime as an ultimate guardian of political stability; second, a system of mixed economy combining market elements with strong governmental regulation for the sake of dynamic development; and third, an official nationalist doctrine, hard enough to be a barrier against communism but soft enough not to hamper foreign investment. Today, in the absence of the Red Threat and in the era of market glorification, AMM with all its past efficiency looks hopelessly outdated. Democratize your politics, demand globalization preachers. Liberalize your economy, forget your nationalism, and be quick — it's easy! Reactions to these demands differ from one Southeast Asian country to the other — with natural consequences for ASEAN's political cohesion and unlikely prospects for anything like a common modernization strategy.

THE QUESTION OF ECONOMIC COMPETITIVENESS

At the dawn of globalization, many of the ASEAN economies seemed to be well schooled in the art of competition on external markets and ready for a new round of it. Since then, however, it has been noted that globalization favours two kinds of market players. Those belonging to the first category are competitive in the realm of post-industrial knowledge-based economy. The representatives of the second category are capable of establishing mass production of exportable consumer goods relying on tested industrial technologies and low-wage workforce. The rapid rise of two Asian giants — China and India — is a major manifestation of these trends. At the same time, globalization is less than friendly to those not fitting any of these groups — in particular, to middle-level economies (just like in the framework of national economies globalization is especially damaging to the middle classes).[2] At present many East European and Latin American countries are on the list of losers, but where is the guarantee that the members of ASEAN, standing at more or less the same level of development, will not eventually join them? Characteristically, the fears of losing international competitiveness — first and foremost to the Chinese and the Indians — are already expressed in public by the association's leaders.[3]

A CUSTODIAN OF REGIONAL BALANCE —
BUT A GLOBAL BULLY, TOO

Perception of the U.S. military presence as an essential element of the Southeast Asian strategic landscape — and, by implication, of regional prosperity — had been at the heart of the ASEAN consensus on security matters for more than three decades. While in a very basic sense this perception is still there, the ambivalence about the regional and the global role of the United States has never been as painful as in the post-Asian Crisis/September 11/Iraqi period. To an ever greater extent, America with its unilateralism and humanitarian interventions is viewed as a force undermining the very fundamentals of the existing world order — a violator of peace and stability, so crucial for successful modernization efforts and sustainable economic growth in Southeast Asia and elsewhere.

WAYS OUT AND STUMBLING BLOCKS

In view of the things said above, what are the primary tasks facing the association and its members today? With the exception of Singapore, they all must continue to modernize at the national levels, and all without exception must join their forces if ASEAN is to be preserved and strengthened as a regional body and a global player. Both types of tasks must be dealt with, to put it mildly, in circumstances not conducive to their solutions. This is especially true about domestic modernizing efforts: A region-wide restoration of AMM is impossible, but full realization of the neoliberal agenda — at least the one resulting in return to a combination of long-term economic dynamism, political stability and a sense of belonging to the Winners Club of the contemporary world — is unrealistic either. On the international front, the situation seems somewhat brighter. Having temporarily lost Indonesia as a core member state, ASEAN is trying to make up for this loss by means of acquiring external "props" — three Northeast Asian nations, its partners in the famous "Ten+3" framework. In principle, the scheme in which ASEAN would be relying on both Japan and China as engines of growth, leaning as an entity towards one of them when having difficulties with the other or mediating between them if they have bilateral problems, seems just what is needed for greater unity and further progress of the association (and a stronger position *vis-à-vis* the United States). However, an overlapping of Japanese economic stagnation, South Korea's preoccupation with the North and China's continued upsurge is spontaneously leading to a transformation of "Ten+3" into "Ten+1", meaning ASEAN plus China. The uneasiness about that turn of things results in attempts to add another element to the projected East Asian Community — India. While some of the ASEAN members see this move as a welcome measure to counter China's growing prominence, Indonesia as ASEAN's own traditional leader feels more and more eclipsed in the company of strong external partners — not a good sign for the future of either the association or the bigger East Asian group.[4] New American attempts to derail the East Asian initiative in a classical divide and rule fashion are to be expected too. By classifying Myanmar as an "outpost of tyranny", Washington is laying ground for intensified pressure not on that country alone, but on the whole of ASEAN (whose other members are not uncritical of Yangon's home policies) and on China (whose military and economic help is of great importance to Myanmar's rulers).[5] Other indications of what may follow in future can be found in the recent publications of Francis Fukuyama.[6] This influential writer believes that the Six-Party Talks on Korean problems involving the United States, China, Japan, Russia, South Korea and North Korea should be transformed into a permanent security body. The latter, says he, may be joined at some point by certain ASEAN members (but, characteristically, not all of them and not the association as a whole). This denial of participation to a respected organization and Fukuyama's clear assumption that the ASEAN Regional Forum (ARF) is not a useful venue for security discussions should neither be missed nor underestimated.

ASEAN AND RUSSIA: WILL THE PARALLELS CROSS?

To a Russian observer of the ASEAN scene a number of comparisons come easily. Like ASEAN, Russia has lost its former modernization model, looks for an adequate substitute and has plenty of proofs that uncritical adoption of neoliberal prescriptions is not the answer. Like ASEAN, Russia is not willing to challenge the U.S. hegemony directly, but is far from happy with the American treatment of the rest of the world. Like ASEAN, Russia is seeking cooperation with China as opposed to economic and strategic dependence on it. Like ASEAN, Russia is contemplating a kind of triangular relationship with China and India as the rising forces of world importance. The parallels are obvious, but once they are drawn one is tempted to remember that in Euclides geometry parallels never cross. Of course, in economics and politics they sometimes do, but never without the determined and enlightened effort of the players. Objectively speaking, both Russia and ASEAN have a stake in each other's recoveries and successes, and each has enough to offer to the other in terms of political, economic and cultural cooperation. What is still missing on both sides is the real sense of the other's importance as a prospective partner, to the point that putting this partner down with disarming frankness is not viewed as something inadmissible even by the statesmen of the highest calibre — such as Lee Kuan Yew who once openly concluded that Russia would not be a major player in world affairs for another twenty years.[7] That was said just five years ago, in 2000. Listening with due respect to a sage like Mr. Lee, why should ASEAN bother at all to have a summit with Russia in 2005, fifteen long years before the earliest "reasonable" date? Does it mean that in the unipolar world, including ASEAN, there is growing demand for a stronger Russia, or Russia is getting its act together quicker than Mr. Lee could have imagined? Let us figure it out by trying to do something useful together.

NOTES

1   ASEAN List of Abbreviations <http://www.aseansec.org/73.htm>.
2   These themes are well presented in Garrett, G., "Globalization's Missing Middle", *Foreign Affairs*, N.Y., November / December 2004.
3   See, for example, Ong Keng Yong, "Advancing ASEAN–EU Relations in the 21st Century", in <http://www.aseansec.org.16536.htm>.
4   Eric Teo Chu Cheow, "East Asia Summit's Birthing Pains", *The Straits Times*, Singapore, 22 February 2005.
5   Bremmer, I., "Bush Signals a Revolution in Foreign Policy", *International Herald Tribune*, 29 January 2005.
6   Fukuyama, F., "Re-Envisioning Asia", *Foreign Affairs*, January/February 2005. A summary of this paper appeared in the *International Herald Tribune* (10 December 2004). An abbreviated Russian translation was published by N.G. Dipkurier of Moscow (7 February 2005).
7   Lee Kuan Yew, "Need for a Balancer on East Asia's Way to World Eminence", *International Herald Tribune*, 23 November 2000.

7

Security Issues in Southeast Asia: Commentary

Andrew Tan Tian Huat

Dr. Victor Sumsky's very interesting presentation raises more questions than it answers, though mostly for good reasons. Beyond the diplomatic, multilateralist and constructivist hype, Dr. Sumsky has detected a dismal picture of emerging security threats from terrorism, piracy, transnational crime, dangerous diseases, economic shocks, the end of the developmental state model so famously pioneered in Asia, the rise of new economic and political great powers, ambivalence about the United States, enduring problems of modernization and the difficulties faced by the ASEAN states in rallying together in order to remain a regional entity and a collective player on the global arena.

Dr. Sumsky's presentation alludes to the two views on contemporary Southeast Asia that is evident in the security literature. The first is obviously the very optimistic constructivist literature that is today dominant in Southeast Asian security, that argues the case for the nascent security community that is evolving within the region. The second view is that of the late Michael Leifer's realist perception of Southeast Asia, best encapsulated in the title of Milton Osborne's book, *A Region of Revolt*, published in 1970. In Leifer's view, norms and multilateralism are important in constructing a better future, but in doing so one should not ignore the very existential problems within the region that continue to persist. These include internal revolts, political instability, armed separatisms and insurgencies that point to a more prescient problem of constructing the state's legitimacy, and of nation-building after decolonization.

Even today, in 2005, one could plausibly make a strong case, as Dr. Sumsky in many ways has, that Southeast Asia remains a problematic region. We see for instance, the continued salience of revolt in places such as Aceh, Malukus, Irian Jaya, Southern Thailand, among the Hmongs, the Karens in Burma, the Moros in Southern Philippines, and the Maoist communist insurgency in the Philippines. In recent days, we have also heard of the naval standoff between Indonesia and Malaysia over a disputed award of an oil concession by Malaysia along their sea border. This sort of thing is not new, as in the 1990s, we have witnessed previous naval standoffs between Thailand and Malaysia, Singapore and Malaysia, and more recently, between Brunei and Malaysia over the Kikeh oil dispute.

Dr. Sumksy wonders about the future of ASEAN and whether it can respond adequately to emerging challenges. In particular, he wonders if ASEAN can remain in the driver's seat, or will the emerging great powers with their strong interest in the region, such as a rising China, an increasingly interested India, a visibly more assertive Japan and a United States that is actively engaged given Southeast Asia's designation as the "second front in the war on terrorism", thwart ASEAN's collective efforts and prevent ASEAN from realizing its objective of an ASEAN community, or indeed, that of an East Asian Community. These great powers, and not just the United States, practise time-honoured divide and rule tactics to gain advantages for themselves and to protect their national interests. As for the ASEAN states themselves, they are not slow to break ranks given the important priority of pursuing their national interests above that of regional ones, should push come to shove.

Witness for instance China's success in preventing any forceful ASEAN consensus on the South China Sea issue and ASEAN's tepid response to the Mischief Reef incident in 1995, when China picked on one of the militarily weakest ASEAN states, the Philippines, to demonstrate its will to maintain its claim over the area. Indeed, the Philippines has capitulated by signing, last year, two agreements permitting joint development in return for an aid package from China. One then cannot be too overly optimistic and I therefore have little to disagree with the general thrust of Dr. Sumsky's presentation.

However, I do have some observations about Russia's role in the region. It is currently virtually a non-role, as it is not a main player unlike China, the United States, Japan and even India. It is also unidimensional in many respects, as the perception of Russia is very much that of an arms supplier to various countries in the region. Russia is still and will remain a formidable great power and will eventually play a greater role in the region but it needs to make its presence felt politically, economically, socially and culturally. I am certain that the region will welcome a much greater visibility on the part of Russia. The more great powers there are, the better, as the region cannot seem to get its act together and in fact threatens to be turned into a Chinese lake in the coming years, as more and more states in the region, with the absence of serious alternatives, bandwagon with China.

Let me now turn to the presentation by Ms. Sidney Jones. Ms. Jones' very useful presentation reminds us of the seriousness of the terrorism problem within the region, particularly the presence of terrorist networks in Indonesia, Philippines and Southern Thailand. Indeed, there is today a consensus that the terrorist problem has not diminished but in fact grown, given the presence of local sources of grievances and conflicts, the lack of legitimacy of central governments over peripheral territories, the continuing challenge of nation-building, the deficiencies in local, regional and international cooperation in the fight against terror networks, and U.S. strategic mistakes in places such as Iraq.

The emergence of the new terrorism motivated by radical Islam has become, and will remain for the foreseeable future, a major security challenge, particularly within the Malay archipelago, which is home to the world's largest population of Muslims and therefore strategically important in the global war against the new terror. Indeed, recent terror attacks in Indonesia and the Philippines, such as the Bali bombing, the Marriott Hotel attack, the attack on the Australian embassy and the Super Ferry sinking in Manila Bay, point to the continuing salience of the threat from the new terrorism.

Yet, it is important to remember that in the Southeast Asian context, the new terrorism was predated by the old terrorism. An older form of ethno-nationalist and political terrorism existed within the region long before Al-Qaeda or Osama bin Laden came into the picture. The presence of fundamental causes of alienation and rebellion amongst Muslims in the region, stemming from long-standing historical, political, economic and social factors, led to the outbreak of rebellions in Indonesia, Philippines and Thailand many years ago, before the new terrorism became in vogue. Even the much vaunted Al-Qaeda linked network, the Jemaah Islamiyah (JI), began as a local group, before Al-Qaeda came into the picture, and many JI activists and operatives in fact belong to families that had taken part in the earlier Darul Islam rebellion in the 1950s.

The difference is that the new terrorism paradigm has meant that some of these disaffected Muslims have now become much better organized, have established regional and international links, raised their technical and operational capabilities, and are motivated by a more forceful and uncompromising brand of pan-Islamic radical ideology. As Ms. Jones rightly pointed out, this calls for better intelligence to deal with the problem. That being said, this better intelligence needs to go beyond merely technical surveillance but must rely more on human intelligence, from actual intelligence gathering to the analysis of intelligence. These call for specialized training and skills, something I am uncertain if academe is actually providing, given the dearth of area studies and of the deep empiricism of the social sciences since 1990.

Another thing that needs to be said about better intelligence is the need to also include better synergies domestically among various security agencies, regionally amongst governments, and internationally amongst nation-states and the international community. However, that is something that will take a great deal of time and effort to evolve and develop. It is a process which we have only just begun; remember that those seminal events on 11 September 2001 occurred just over three-and-a-half years ago.

Finally, on top of better intelligence, the presence of long-standing fundamental causes also point, as Ms. Jones has rightly done, to the need for governments in the region to put a higher priority on understanding, resolving and preventing local conflicts, something which requires, in the long-run, far-sighted political solutions.

Given the plethora of security problems stemming from conflict and violence in the region, what is needed is excellent strategic thinking and foresight on the part of the region's analysts, policymakers and statesmen. Sadly, this is becoming a lost art as the older generation of independence leaders have vacated the scene, and intellectually, we have lost our empirical and realist bearing. Correct me if I am wrong, but Southeast Asia faces grave challenges ahead.

PART IV
Bilateral Economic Relations

⑧
Singapore-Russia Economic Relations

Aw Siew Juan

IE Singapore started its office in Moscow with a local commercial secretary in 1997. Later, an honorary business advisor, Mr. Rajinder Sethi, was appointed to help IE Singapore understand the complexities of business practices in Russia, as well as to harness the opportunities that might arise.

OVERVIEW OF RUSSIA'S ECONOMY SINCE THE 1990s

Legacy of a State-Run Economy

As a result of its Soviet central planning legacy and rich resource endowments, Russia's industrial sector is heavily skewed towards heavy industries. In 2002 machine-building and metal-working remained the largest processing industry, accounting for just over 20 per cent of industrial production. Light industry — which includes textiles — accounted for only 1.5 per cent of industrial output.

That Russia's economy is very much dominated by the mining industry is demonstrated by the fact that, in an October 2004 ranking of top 400 Russian companies, 266 companies were connected with mining of natural resources. These companies accounted for 74 per cent of the Top-400 aggregate revenue. In contrast, there were only fifty-six companies of the "new economy"

— banks, insurers and IT companies, cellular operators, retail networks and newly created industrial enterprises.

Market Reforms

The transition from a highly-industrialized command economy to a market-based economy has been taking place since 1991, boosting private consumption and benefiting all sectors of the economy that cater to consumers. Retailers, communications service providers, car dealers, car maintenance services, insurers, dealers of branded consumer durables, producers of personal care and fitness services are segments where significant growth is expected for several years.

Russia's Hopes of WTO Accession

Since China's accession to the WTO in 2001, Russia is the largest economy that is not yet a part of this global trade forum. Russia began its drawn-out WTO accession process some eleven years ago. However, services continues to be a sticking point, with Russia unwilling to further open up its banking and insurance sectors — a key U.S. demand. The United States has also expressed concerns over Russia's dual energy pricing policy under which domestic prices amount to approximately one-fourth of export prices. Several WTO members have charged that these prices constitute a *de facto* subsidy to Russian industry, although the EU did not take a hardline stance on the matter when signing its bilateral agreement with Russia in May 2004.

Accession to the WTO would help make Russia's economy more transparent and predictable, increase the protection of minority shareholder rights, and strengthen the enforcement of contracts.

Oil-Led Growth

Since President Putin took office in 2000, a wide-ranging market-based structural reform programme has been on-going. Some of the key reforms introduced over the past years include the bankruptcy code (1998), flat personal income tax rate (13 per cent) and a new corporate rate (20 per cent) and land code. While the high energy prices in the last few years no doubt helped to boost GDP figures, these reforms have nonetheless contributed to Russia's impressive GDP growth over the last six years (Figure 8.1).

After emerging from the rouble crisis of 1998, Russia has averaged 6.7 per cent real GDP growth per annum. Latest reports indicate that the country has also achieved about 7 per cent GDP growth in 2004.

Figure 8.1
GDP of Russia (1994–2004)

US$ (billion)

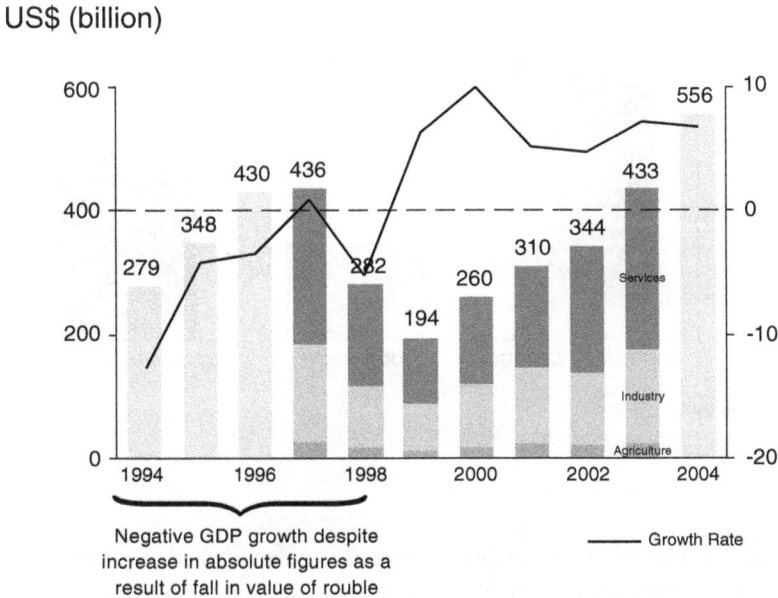

Negative GDP growth despite
increase in absolute figures as a
result of fall in value of rouble

———— Growth Rate

Table 8.1

Ratings Agency	Rating
Moody's sovereign debt ratings (Oct 2003)	Baa3
Fitch sovereign debt ratings (Nov 2003)	BBB-
S&P's sovereign debt ratings (Jan 2005)	BBB-

Russia's track record over the last six to seven years has not gone unnoticed. As of January 2005, the three top ratings agencies have all awarded Russia with long-term sovereign debt ratings in the investment grade category (Table 8.1).

Russia's Trade and Foreign Direct Investment

In 2004, Russia's imports were dominated by intermediate/downstream industrial products and foodstuffs (Figure 8.2). Demand for food imports

Figure 8.2
Russia's Trade Pattern By Product (2004)

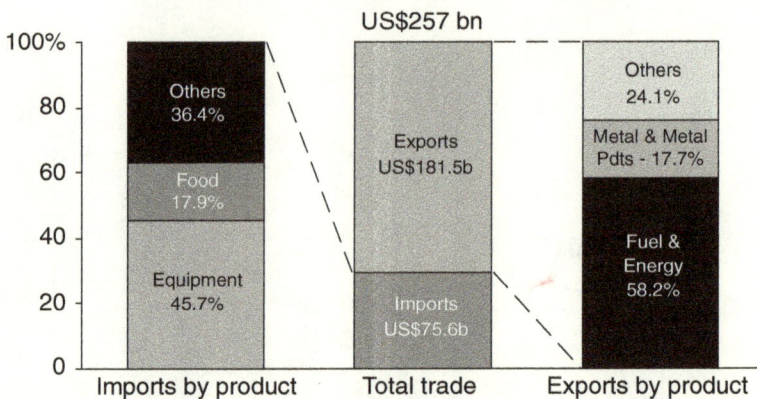

Source: Factiva

was also substantial due to the weak state of Russian agriculture and consumer demands for new tastes which the domestic industry cannot fulfil. Close to 60 per cent of Russia's total earnings came from fuel and energy, with metals accounting for a further 17.7 per cent, leaving Russia's trade balance vulnerable to volatility of international commodities prices.

Russia's current-account surplus reached a record US$58 billion in 2004. A 62 per cent increase on the 2003 figure, this was much higher than the previous record surplus of US$46.8 billion recorded in 2000. Very high oil prices meant that revenue from crude oil exports grew by over 48 per cent year-on-year in U.S. dollar terms, leading to an overall rise in goods exports by 34 per cent. As a result, the goods trade surplus increased by 44 per cent, to over US$87 billion, despite growth of around 25 per cent in imports driven by brisk domestic demand growth and real rouble appreciation, as well as the weakness of the U.S. dollar against the euro.

As international oil prices ease in 2005–06, the current-account surplus is projected to more than halve in relative terms, from around 10 per cent of GDP in 2004 to just over 4 per cent of GDP in 2006.

Singapore's trade with Russia somewhat mirrors Russia's overall trade pattern. Our exports to Russia are dominated by machinery and electronics, while fuel and mineral ores form the bulk of our imports from Russia (Figure 8.3).

Figure 8.3
Singapore's Trade with Russia (2004)

S$ (thousand)

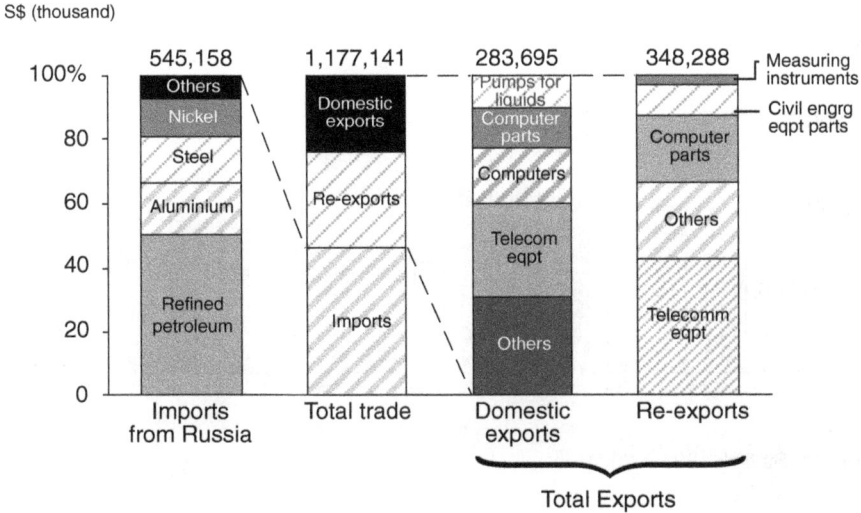

Source: Statlink

Following in the footsteps of Russia's GDP growth, Singapore's exports to Russia have also increased steadily. From 1999–2004, our exports to Russia have jumped from S$455 million to S$1.18 billion (Figure 8.4). However, Singapore's trade with Russia (as a proportion of Russia's total trade) has hardly moved. Over the last five years, Singapore has accounted for a mere 0.25 per cent of Russia's total trade. This gives rise to a lot of potential for Singapore companies to do more business with Russia.

Foreign Direct Investment in Russia

Cumulative FDI inflows in Russia from 1990 up to the end of 2003 of just over US$28 billion were equal to only 6.5 per cent of GDP, the lowest share among all 27 countries of the transition region, and one-fifth of the average penetration ratio in East-Central Europe. Russia's share in the transition region's population, GDP and exports is about one-third; its share in the region's stock of FDI is below 13 per cent.

Although reforms of the tax regime and the new-found political and economic stability have improved the investment climate, much remains to be done in the areas of enforcement and implementation of policies to reduce

Figure 8.4
Singapore's Trade with Russia (1992–2004)

S$

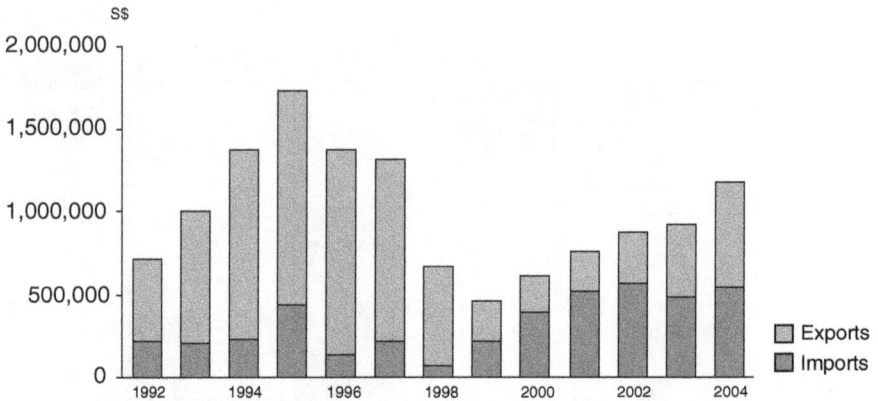

Source: Statlink 1992 – 2004

operational risks for businesses. Today businesses in Russia struggle with unclear and overbearing regulation, arbitrary administrative decisions, corrupt officials and biased or incompetent judges.

BUSINESS OPPORTUNITIES IN KEY SECTORS

Oil and Gas

Russia is important to world energy markets as it holds the world's largest natural gas reserves and the eighth largest oil reserves. It is also the world's largest exporter of natural gas and second largest oil exporter, after Saudi Arabia.

Russia's huge oil reserves are distributed unevenly. Most of the huge reserves are now offshore (the Arctic shelf, the Far Eastern shelf, the Azov and Caspian sea shelves), needing huge investment and high technology. Increasingly Russian oil majors are now conducting more exploration in West Siberia, in the Russian sector of the Caspian Sea and joining forces with foreign oil producers to develop oil projects in the Russian Far East and Sakhalin Island.

The market for oil and gas equipment and services was worth US$1.76 billion in 2002, of which 46 per cent was imported. This presents opportunities

Figure 8.5
Russian Market for Oil and Gas Equipment and Services

US$ million

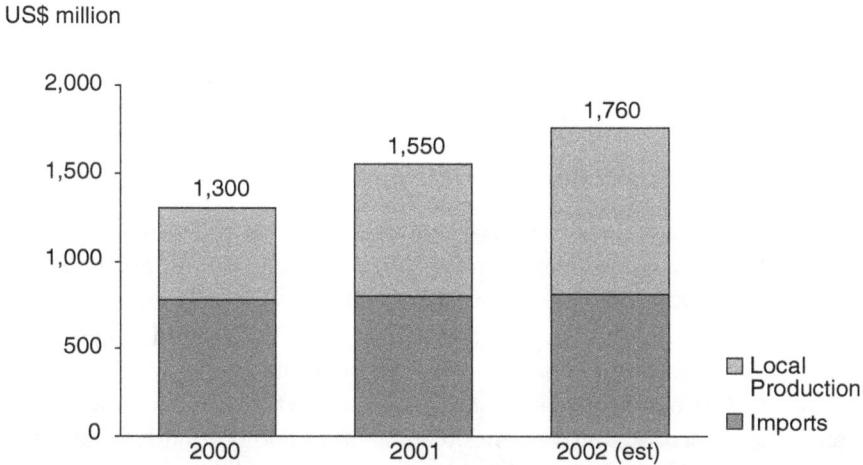

Source: STAT-USA Russia Country Commercial Guide 2003

for Singapore companies to supply offshore platforms and pipelines, as well as provide bunkering and other maritime services.

Retail

Since 2000, retail sales has been growing at an average of 9 per cent a year, reaching US$170 billion in 2003. This trend is expected to continue, boosting sales to at least US$204 billion by 2008. This can be attributed to low income taxes (13 per cent on average), and the fact that the majority of Russians pay little or no rent as a result of Soviet-era housing programmes, which translate to high levels of disposable income. Disposable income is predicted to further increase by 46 per cent in 2010.

All segments of the consumer goods market are expected to grow fairly rapidly over the medium term (2003–07). Many retail chains have also announced plans to open chains of stores, with a trend towards opening of supermarkets and hypermarkets in the major cities.

With Russians known for having adventurous appetites, Singapore companies should consider introducing their oriental blend of processed food to the Russian consumers. Many wholly Russian-owned plants may not be up to global production and health standards. Singapore companies can exploit this opportunity to penetrate the Russian market by partnering or acquiring local companies. There is also increasing demand for restaurants and entertainment in the major cities.

Russia is also interesting for consumer electronics companies, especially with a growing Russian middle class that wishes to attain the luxuries of a Western lifestyle.

Real Estate and Property Development

In 2003, a shortage of commercial and residential space in major Russian cities pushed average residential and office property prices up by 20–25 per cent to US$1,200–4,000 per square metre. This has brought property prices in cities like Moscow and St. Petersburg close to New York and Tokyo levels, making them one of the most expensive cities in the world.

Buoyant demand for residential apartments has turned Moscow and St. Petersburg into a busy construction site. In good locations, residential property prices can fetch US$4,000–9,000 per square metre, while costs for high class developments still remain between US$1,200–1,500 per square metre. Projects are also increasingly equipped with modern features such as flexible floor space, modern infrastructure, quality engineering, basement parking and security systems.

While there are sufficient four to five-star hotels in key cities like Moscow and St. Petersburg, there is a shortage of three-star hotels catering to business travellers seeking quality, reasonably-priced accommodation with good service standards (Figure 8.6).

Regional governments are also increasingly relocating industries to satellite towns in order to reduce congestion in the main cities. Such exercises free up attractive land in the city centre for investment and redevelopment, and present opportunities for Singapore companies to be involved in township design and planning, as well as the building and management of industrial parks.

Automotive Components

Russia has the ninth largest car market in the world, with 98,000 additional cars expected to be placed on the road every year till 2014. In 2004, the country produced about 1.11 million cars, of which 133,000 was produced by foreign joint ventures. The increasing number of foreign car manufacturers moving to Russia (for example, Opel, Ford, Kia), coupled with the growing sales of foreign-brand cars, points to a growing Russian appetite for better quality cars, which in turn need quality components.

Figure 8.6
Distribution of Tourists, Hotels and Hotel Rooms (2003 – Estimate)

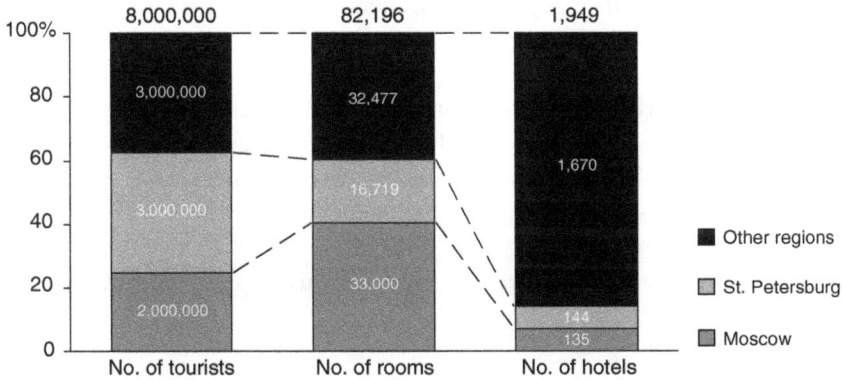

Source: Hotel Market Trends (September 2003), U.S. Dept. of State Commercial Service
       Russia: Tourism Background (January 2004), EIU.

The Russian auto components industry is badly in need of revitalization. Local manufacturers continue to churn out parts using equipment dating as far back as the 1930s. According to the Moscow Chamber of Commerce, Russian companies possess the necessary expertise to produce high-tech components (having won seventy per cent of the medals at a Brussels exhibition of high-tech companies). What they lack is the funds to upgrade their obsolete equipment in order to produce high-quality components.

With its 145 million population, steady economic growth and rising purchasing power, Russia is becoming a promising market for car and auto component makers. Herein lies the opportunity for Singapore companies to penetrate the Russian auto parts market, worth an estimated US$10.2 billion annually, either through acquisitions or joint ventures with Russian SMEs.

CONCLUSION

While there are undoubtedly problems with doing business in Russia, the same could be said of other transitional and emerging economies. This, however, presents an opportunity for companies to create that first mover advantage by introducing new and better products and services. For several companies that ventured there many years ago, patience and hard work has paid off in the form of significant earnings and sustainable growth. Now, companies like Amtel and Food Empire are savouring the rewards of their early efforts, with both being market leaders in their respective sectors.

Given the relative stability of the new Putin administration, the various economic reforms that are taking place, as well as Russia's eagerness to integrate itself with the global economy with impending entry into the WTO, Singapore companies should seriously consider Russia, with its population of 144 million, as an alternative business and investment destination.

Note: This chapter includes excerpts from an earlier presentation.

⑨
Russia-Singapore Relations: Thirty-seven Years of Cooperation and Dialogue

Mark Hong

HISTORY BACKGROUND

Singapore and the former Soviet Union established full diplomatic relations on 1 June 1968. A joint statement described the moves as a "further step towards maintaining close and friendly relations" between both countries. Singapore's first Prime Minister, Mr Lee Kuan Yew visited Moscow in 1962, even before Singapore became independent in August 1965, to lobby for Soviet support for the creation of Malaysia, of which Singapore was a member from 1963–65. In November 1965, Singapore's then Deputy Prime Minister, Dr Toh Chin Chye, made the first official visit to the former Soviet Union. Following Dr Toh's visit, a Trade Agreement was signed in April 1966. Trade Representation Offices were subsequently established in Moscow and Singapore. The first Soviet Ambassador to Singapore, Mr Ilya I. Safronovich, was appointed in January 1969. Singapore appointed its first Ambassador to the former Soviet Union, the late Mr P. S. Raman, in July 1971.

High level official visitors from Singapore have included Mr Lee Kuan Yew (1990) and the Speaker of Parliament, Mr Tan Soo Khoon (1997), Foreign Minister Prof. S. Jayakumar in September 2002, Minister for Trade and Industry George Yeo in 2004, whilst several Russian Ministers have visited Singapore, such as Foreign Ministers Primakov and Igor Ivanov for the ASEAN Post Ministerial meetings. The most recent visit was in October 2003, by F.M. Ivanov.

During the Cold War era, Singapore pragmatically continued to cooperate with the USSR in trade and economic cooperation, by forming several joint ventures. From independence in 1965, Singapore had felt that the USSR could play a role in the power-balance in Southeast Asia, but this view changed after the signing of the Soviet-Vietnam Treaty of Friendship and Cooperation in 1978, and the establishment of a Soviet naval base in Camranh Bay in Vietnam, and the Soviet support given to Vietnam for its invasion and occupation of Cambodia, seen as a threat to regional security. In 1989, in line with the new economic diplomacy policy and with the ending of the Cambodian conflict and the end of the Cold War, Singapore announced its intention to expand economic ties with China and the USSR.

Singapore had always been pragmatic about the Soviet Union in its economic cooperation, thus allowing the Moscow Narodny Bank to open a branch in Singapore, having Soviet ships repaired in Singapore and also allowing Aeroflot to fly to Singapore.

BILATERAL TRADE

Trade was another area of cooperation. In 1968, the total bilateral trade between both countries amounted to only S$140 million. Ten years later in 1978, the figure had more than doubled to S$311 million. Growth thereafter was much slower. By 1988, it had only increased to S$446 million. But the development of a market economy in Russia, and the recovery from the rouble crash as well as from the Asian financial crisis, has given a boost to bilateral trade. As of 2004, the total trade amounted to S$1.17 billion, almost triple the figure of a decade earlier. Our exports to Russia totalled S$600m. Singapore is now the largest trading partner of Russia amongst the ASEAN countries, even though it was only the 40th largest trading partner. In 2002, bilateral trade had amounted to $880 million (Singapore's exports totalled $310m, imports totalled $569m). The impact of the Asian and Russian economic crises had thus reduced the annual trade figures. But after the crisis, bilateral trade gradually recovered. Singapore has sent annual trade delegations to visit Russia in order to increase trade and has also set up a trade office at the Singapore Embassy in Moscow. Singapore's investments in Russia totalled US$770 million by June 2003. In 2004, the Singapore Business Federation concluded a MOU with OPORA Russia, which represents Russian small and medium enterprises. Also in December 2004, Temasek bought a 2.6% stake worth S$500m in Russia's Mobile TeleSystems. The Singapore Business Federation hosted a Russia Business Round Table in March 2005 to promote bilateral business ties, and will lead a business delegation to visit Russia in May 2005.

JOINT VENTURES

In February 1968, SOSIAC (Singapore-Soviet Shipping Company Pte Limited) was established as the first Singapore-Soviet joint venture. Today, Russian and Singapore joint ventures are numerous, working together in a wide variety of areas. Many Singapore companies operate in contemporary Russia, such as Amtel, Acma, Thakral, Swissotel, Upasana, Pakson Electronics, International Bearings, Kwangsia. Their activities range from consumer electronics, tyre production, tourism, timber products, and food to oil exploration and deep-sea fishing. Russian companies that operate in Singapore include Lukoil, Sinsov, Moscow Narodny Bank and Agrosin.

Negotiations on a Double Taxation Agreement began in 1972, when economic relations between the former Soviet Union and Singapore were at an early stage of development. In view of the increasing economic ties, the signing of the DTA agreement in 2002 was a positive and necessary step. Similarly, as the amount and range of Singapore investments in Russia continues to grow, an Investment Guarantee Agreement is being discussed. The DTA agreements were signed during FM Jayakumar's visit to Moscow in 2002. One earlier economic agreement signed in 1998 was a Memorandum of Understanding between the former Singapore Productivity and Standards Board and the Russian State Committee for Standardisation, Metrology and Certification, or Goostandart.

Economic relations have thus provided the foundation of our relationship for 37 years. There is great potential for the further development of economic cooperation, particularly between the private sectors. Tourism is another area with great potential for growth and STB is interested to increase high-yield Russian tourism to Singapore. With the start of Transaero flights to Singapore, the air links have been restored, since Aeroflot flights from Moscow to Singapore had stopped.

There is potential in other areas as well. Russia has a rich cultural heritage, which Singapore has tapped. Singapore and the former Soviet

Union had concluded several agreements on cultural cooperation. This was revived when Singapore and Russia signed a Cultural Memorandum of Understanding in May 1994. Since then a number of well-known artistes and troupes have performed at the annual Singapore Arts Festival. These include the Moscow State Symphony Orchestra, the Alexandrov Red Army Ensemble and the St. Petersburg Philharmonic Orchestra.

Russia also has a wealth of advanced science and technology. This is another rich area that can be developed for mutual benefit. The National University of Singapore has launched an Eastern Europe Research Scientists and Students Exchange Programme, which also include Russian scientists. The NUS Mathematical Sciences Institute has an exchange programme with the maths department of Moscow State University. Another Singapore university, Nanyang Technological University, has signed an agreement to offer a double Masters degree in computer engineering with the Moscow Institute of Physics and Technology. There is thus potential synergy between Russian technology and Singapore's knowledge of commercial markets, which was symbolised by the MoU signed in May 2002 between the Russian Union of Manufacturers and Entrepreneurs and the Singapore Confederation of Industrialists. Russian Sukhoi defence plants were bidding for the contract to replace Singapore's ageing A4 Skyhawks fighters, but later dropped out.

The beginning of the new 21st century and the start of President Putin's era have enabled further development of relations. Under the strong leadership of Mr Putin, Russia has regained political stability and steady economic growth, which makes Russia an inviting market and economic partner for Singapore, which needs new markets. Singapore and Russia today not only cooperate bilaterally, but also under the auspices of the ASEAN-Russia Dialogue, the ASEAN Post Ministerial Conferences, the ASEAN Regional Forum, the Shangri-la defence ministers dialogue and in APEC. Russia's membership of these regional organizations reflects its growing integration with the Asia-Pacific region. Both countries share common interests in promoting Asia-Pacific growth and stability.

Since the 1990s, with the rise of India and China, the boom in Asia has continued and expanded. Russia and Siberia lie just to the north of the Asian boom, and observers wonder how and where would Russia fit in. Would Moscow look only towards the west, towards the EU, or would Siberia be drawn southwards, especially as new oil pipelines, road and rail links with China and Korea are built. The dynamic growth of China would increasingly attract the rich natural resources found in Siberia and Maritime Far East, particularly energy and raw materials. Then there is the question of economic and political cooperation which is being built under various forums, such as the ASEAN+3, the East Asian Summit, and JACIK. Russia is closely monitoring such developments, and its participation level will increase in late 2005, when President Putin attends the Russia-ASEAN Summit in Kuala Lumpur.

Singapore is actively looking for new markets. As Siberian cities lie within the six-hour flying time radius from Singapore, inevitably our businessmen will explore Russian markets, even as they look at North Chinese provinces, lying next to Siberia. The forces of the free market will help to integrate North China, Siberia and ASEAN countries, through such agencies as budget airlines. Chinese budget airlines will link both Siberia and ASEAN through Chinese cities such as Shanghai and Beijing.

As airlinks grow, adventure travel and eco-tourism will take off. Ordinary people will be richer because of the Asian boom, and having visited the cities of the region, the tourists would want to see something different: unspoilt nature, in Siberia and Kamchatka. Climate change may also change the severe climate of Siberia and turn it to a warmer, more welcoming weather for tourists to ski and take winter holidays. Tourists will also be looking north, especially after the 2008 Beijing Olympics, and if the rail links are ready in time, with good connections to the Trans-Siberian railway, the mystique of this romantic journey to Moscow through "the snows of Dr. Zhivago" will draw the young and romantic. Better transport will move more people and cargo across north Asia. The forces of globalization and modernization will increasingly inter-connect the various peoples of Asia as the political and economic linkages are being built.

Russia may not be used to cooperating with a city-state such as Singapore. But it is not so much the size of territory that counts but also the quality of ideas and the excellence of governance and economic management that Singapore has demonstrated. For instance, in 2005, Russia and Singapore agreed to jointly set up industrial parks within Russia, thus tapping the rich experience of Singapore in this area. The strength and resilience of Singapore's political and socio-economic systems have been clearly demonstrated in the 1997–98 Asian economic and financial crises, and in fighting terrorism and SARS. Singapore is now concentrating on building a knowledge economy and restructuring its economy to face challenges posed by China. Singapore has advanced Information Technology and is focussing on sectors such as life sciences, education and medical services. There is much potential for cooperation between Russia and Singapore, once the obstacles of mutual ignorance, language differences, distance and insufficient contacts have been overcome.

10

Rationale for a Free Trade Agreement between Russia and Singapore and Russia-ASEAN

Rahul Sen

INTRODUCTION

Free Trade Agreements (FTAs) are an instrument of regionalism, defined as "actions by governments to liberalize or facilitate trade on a preferential basis". It is one of the most elementary forms of regionalism. In recent years, the scope of these FTAs has ranged from being cross-regional or even inter-continental, to individual countries/regional groupings. The recent wave of FTAs emerging in Asia has been more comprehensive, with a wider coverage beyond tariff reductions covering trade in services, investments and regulatory measures to facilitate and promote trade and investment flows.

Essentially, FTAs are meant to reduce business costs and facilitate market access to member countries. An FTA thus provides benefits to its member countries in terms of removal of barriers to trade and investment flows among them, and enhancing the market access for goods exporters as well as for service providers from these countries, as well as expanding investment opportunities abroad. It also serves to strengthen strategic partnership between the member countries.

However, it is important to note that entering into FTAs also requires adjustments to the domestic economy of FTA partners, since it generates greater competition in the domestic economy. Also, FTAs enforce policy discipline, as policy changes are "locked in" through liberalization commitments in these agreements. Further, domestic businesses may also need to adjust their operations to succeed in overseas markets of FTA members that may be highly competitive.

The remainder of this chapter analyses the rationale for a free trade agreement between Singapore and Russia, and also between Russia and ASEAN. The next section briefly discusses the motivations behind Singapore's FTAs and their current status. The final section analyses the rationale for a Singapore-Russia FTA and the possibilities of it being a pathfinder for an ASEAN-Russia FTA, and concludes the chapter.

SINGAPORE'S FTA STRATEGY

Singapore is a small, open economy whose trade policy directions are underpinned by its dependence on the global economy, and the constraints of a small domestic market with limited natural resources. Being a manufacturing and trading hub for Southeast Asia, Singapore is one of the most open economies in the region with a trade-to-GDP ratio of over 250 per cent in recent years. Therefore, international trade policy remains the cornerstone in defining the shape of Singapore's economic success, and that Singapore policymakers have been consciously attempting to find ways and means towards achieving freer trade in East Asia.

Singapore's rationale for pursuing FTAs has been manifold. As observed by Liang (2005):[1]

> FTAs can provide impetus to multilateral trade liberalisation; identify compatible partners with whom to pursue faster and broader liberalisation, thus acting as catalyst for multilateral trade liberalisation...FTAs create positive competitive dynamics that spur further liberalisation.... FTAs put pressure on those that are slow to liberalise and in the process, help to push everyone towards liberalisation at the regional and multilateral level. FTAs engender the internal economic reform processes.... FTAs can help governments to overcome domestic resistance to reforms of sensitive sectors. Governments may be more willing to initiate difficult domestic reforms if they can be carried out on a preferential basis and in measured steps. FTAs improve the economic competitiveness of businesses and provide greater access to the markets of FTA partners.

Singapore's motivations for entering into FTAs stemmed from the limited progress on WTO negotiations and the onset of the economic crisis in East Asia in 1997–98, which slowed down ASEAN's growth momentum. The continuing slow progress at the multilateral level prompted Singapore to look for alternative means towards achieving liberalizing trade and investment within the global economy, and it is against this backdrop that Singapore has been actively pursuing bilateralism through negotiation of FTAs as a key strategy of its commercial trade policy.

There has been a two-pronged strategy by Singapore policymakers with respect to entering into FTAs:

a) To deepen economic linkages with its important trading partners.
b) To enhance market access in new and emerging markets, which are not major trading partners of Singapore.

Towards this goal, Singapore has already concluded FTAs with New Zealand (entered into force on 1 January 2001), Japan (in force 30 November 2002), EFTA (European Free Trade Association comprising Switzerland, Iceland, Liechtenstein and Norway) (in force 1 January 2003), Australia (in force 28 July 2003), the United States (in force 1 January 2004,) Jordan (in force early 2005), South Korea (signed in April 2005), and Trans-Pacific Strategic Economic Partnership (SEP) Agreement involving Singapore, Brunei, Chile and New Zealand (signed in July 2005) and India (in force from August 2005). Singapore is currently engaged in FTA negotiations with Canada, Mexico, Panama, Sri Lanka, Qatar, Kuwait, Peru, Bahrain, Egypt, and the UAE. All these initiatives will result in opening up markets in the Americas, Middle East, South Asia, as well as North Asia. All FTAs aimed to be comprehensive and WTO-plus, covering the main areas of trade in goods, services, contingency measures, trade facilitation, investment, government procurement, competition policy and protection of intellectual property rights.

In spite of these moves towards FTAs, Singapore remains committed to multilateral free trade. It is an active participant in the WTO and remains hopeful for a successful Doha round.

RATIONALE FOR A RUSSIA-SINGAPORE FTA AND A RUSSIA-ASEAN FTA

Russia is projected to be a major economic power in the coming decades (it has been mentioned among the BRIC economies (Brazil, Russia, India, China) that would be a major global economic power by 2050). Singapore is one of the most open economies, and a major trading and manufacturing hub in the region, and can provide a gateway for Russia to expand its economic linkages in Southeast Asia through a possible FTA. Further, a Russia-Singapore FTA would also help Singapore to expand its linkages in Central Asia, and also facilitate Russia to tap into Singapore's existing FTA network to expand its market access beyond Southeast Asia.

In the above manner, a Singapore-Russia FTA may eventually evolve as a "pathfinder" for a Russia-ASEAN FTA. ASEAN is already negotiating bilateral FTAs with its major dialogue partners *viz.* China, India, Japan, Korea, as well as Australia and New Zealand. Russia is another important dialogue partner of ASEAN, which might also contemplate entering into a similar agreement with ASEAN, in order to deepen its economic and strategic links with ASEAN member countries.

Indeed, without an FTA with ASEAN, Russia may be left out of this evolving community of FTAs in ASEAN. Its businesses would therefore be deprived of a preferential access to services and investments in a market of 500 million ASEAN consumers. Thus, it can be argued that a strong rationale does exists for Russia to consider an FTA with Singapore, and eventually, with ASEAN.

However, it is important for Russia that it should join the WTO before embarking on bilateral/regional FTAs. This will facilitate its FTA negotiations that are guided by the WTO principles. Further, as noted by Sen (2004),[2] both sides would need to understand the exact nature of the gains from trade from entering into such agreements, which would be vital to the success of the FTA.

NOTES

1   Liang, Margaret, "Singapore's Trade Policies: Priorities and Options", *ASEAN Economic Bulletin* 22, no. 1 (2005): 49–59.
2   Sen, Rahul, "Free Trade Agreements in Southeast Asia", *Southeast Asia Background Series no. 1*, Singapore: ISEAS, 2004.

11
Russia-ASEAN: Problems and Prospects of Economic Cooperation

Viacheslav B. Amirov

To assess the prospects of economic cooperation between Russia and ASEAN, it is necessary first of all to look at the current state of economic interaction between Russia and individual members of ASEAN as well as between Russia and ASEAN as an economic entity. Even after a quick glance, it is easy to see that since the beginning of the 1990s Russia and ASEAN have, in general, developed their political dialogue and political relations quite successfully. On the other hand, the achieved level of Russia's bilateral economic ties with the leading members of ASEAN and consequently with ASEAN as a sub-regional group cannot be described as satisfactory, to put it mildly.

It is natural that Russia's economic relations with various members of ASEAN differ taking into account the history of Southeast Asia during several decades of the Cold War when the region was divided into two blocks along ideological lines. Consequences of that division are still felt in political and economic ties between Russia and ASEAN member-states. In particular it has affected economic exchanges or limited the development of interaction between Russia and some of the founding members of ASEAN.

TRADE

Volume of trade is the most obvious indicator of the current state of economic relations between Russia and ASEAN. Tables 11.1–11.3 clearly show that ASEAN occupies a very low place in Russia's foreign trade, be it in its export or in its import. Since a fall in the Russia-ASEAN trade as a result of the 1998 East Asian financial crisis and a similar one in Russia, there has been a recovery in bilateral trade but its significance is still very low for both sides. There are no members of ASEAN among main Russian trading partners and *vice versa* —Russia is not a main source of any imports for ASEAN countries nor is it a significant export market for goods made in Southeast Asia.

Comparing Russia's trade with Northeast Asia and Southeast Asia, Russia's trade with China has been constantly growing recently and has probably reached US$20 billion in 2004 if the estimated volume of "shuttle-trade" is added to the official trade figures (see Table 11.3). Russia's trade with Japan has also been rapidly recovering during the last two years after its decline and stagnation in the 1990s. The volume of trade between the two countries climbed up to US$7.5 billion (according to Japanese statistics, it even exceeded US$8 billion) in 2004. Either of the two figures is higher than the peak of US$6.2 billion reached in the Soviet-Japanese bilateral trade at the end of the 1980s. Overall, Russia's trade with NEA-3 (China, Japan and South Korea) stands at more than US$30 billion (2004) compared to the total volume of Russia-ASEAN trade which is estimated at between US$3.0–3.5 billion only.

These figures show conclusively that development of Russia-ASEAN economic ties is lagging substantially behind the progress made between them in political relations since the beginning of the last decade.

Among members of ASEAN, Malaysia, Singapore (despite the bad year of 2003, Russia-Singapore trade is back on track in 2004 according to the preliminary data) and Vietnam are currently the most important partners for Russia (Table 11.4).

Vietnam and Singapore are traditional economic partners of Russia (for various reasons) compared to Malaysia, which is a rather new one.

Russia-Vietnam economic ties have been considerably reduced due to the changed nature of relationship between the two countries after the disintegration of the USSR. Though Vietnam is no longer the only valuable and best ally of Russia in East Asia, it continues to be a very important and friendly partner (the relations are even termed strategic partnership). The existing potential for recovering bilateral economic ties (albeit in new forms of trade and investment exchanges) under new circumstances is quite substantial, although to realize this will require significant efforts from both

Table 11.1
Top Ten Partners of Russia in its Export (US$ billion)

Countries	1997	1998	1999	2000	2001	2002	2003	2004ˣ
Netherlands	4.6 (5)	3.9 (5)	3.7 (6)	4.3 (9)	4.7 (6)	7.5 (2)	8.7 (2)	15.2 (1)
Germany	6.6 (2)	5.7 (1)	6.2 (1)	9.2 (1)	9.2 (1)	8.1 (1)	10.4 (1)	13.2 (2)
Italy	3.6 (7)	3.2 (6)	3.8 (5)	7.3 (2)	7.4 (2)	7.4 (3)	8.5 (3)	12.2 (3)
Belarus	4.6 (4)	4.7 (4)	3.8 (4)	5.6 (3)	5.3 (4)	5.9 (5)	7.6 (6)	11.1 (4)
Ukraine	7.2 (1)	5.6 (2)	4.8 (2)	5.0 (5)	5.3 (5)	5.9 (6)	7.6 (5)	10.7 (5)
China	4.0 (6)	3.2 (7)	3.5 (7)	5.2 (4)	5.9 (3)	6.8 (4)	8.2 (4)	10.2 (6)
Turkey	–	–	–	–	3.2 (10)	–	4.8 (9)	7.4 (7)
USA	4.8 (3)	5.1 (3)	4.7 (3)	4.6 (7)	4.2 (9)	4.0 (8)	–	6.5 (8)
Kazakhstan	–	–	–	–	–	–	–	4.7 (9)
Japan	3.1 (9)	–	–	–	–	–	–	3.4 (10)
U.K.	2.9 (10)	3.0 (9)	2.9 (9)	4.7 (6)	4.3 (7)	3.8 (9)	4.9 (8)	–
Poland	–	2.2 (10)	2.6 (10)	4.5 (8)	4.2 (8)	3.7 (10)	4.6 (10)	–
Switzerland	3.6 (8)	3.1 (8)	3.4 (8)	3.9 (10)	–	5.4 (7)	5.8 (7)	–
ASEAN-6	**1.0**	**0.5**	**0.9**	**1.1**	**1.2**	**1.4**	**1.5**	**...**
Total	86.1	71.3	72.9	103.1	100.0	106.2	133.4	181.5

ˣ Preliminary data ** in brackets – place
Source: Russian Federation Custom Statistics of Foreign Trade.

Table 11.2
Top Ten Partners of Russia in its Import (US$ billion)

Countries	1997	1998	1999	2000	2001	2002	2003	2004ˣ
Germany	6.7 (1)	5.5 (1)	4.2 (1)	3.9 (1)	5.8 (1)	6.6 (1)	8.1 (1)	10.6 (1)
Belarus	4.6 (2)	4.6 (2)	3.2 (2)	3.7 (2)	4.0 (2)	4.0 (2)	4.9 (2)	6.5 (2)
Ukraine	4.0 (4)	3.3 (4)	2.5 (3)	3.6 (3)	3.8 (3)	3.2 (3)	4.4 (3)	6.1 (3)
China	–	1.2 (10)	0.9 (9)	0.9 (9)	1.6 (7)	2.4 (5)	3.3 (4)	4.8 (4)
Japan	–	–	–	–	–	–	1.9 (9)	3.9 (5)
Kazakhstan	2.7 (5)	1.9 (5)	1.4 (5)	2.2 (5)	2.0 (5)	1.9 (7)	2.5 (6)	3.5 (6)
USA	4.1 (3)	4.1 (3)	2.4 (4)	2.7 (4)	3.2 (4)	3.0 (4)	3.0 (5)	3.2 (7)
Italy	2.6 (6)	1.8 (6)	1.2 (7)	1.2 (6)	1.7 (6)	2.2 (6)	2.4 (7)	3.2 (8)
France	1.6 (8)	1.6 (7)	1.2 (6)	1.2 (7)	1.5 (8)	1.9 (8)	2.3 (8)	–
Finland	1.9 (7)	1.4 (8)	0.9 (8)	1.0 (8)	1.3 (9)	1.5 (9)	1.8 (10)	–
U.K.	1.5 (9)	1.2 (9)	–	0.9 (10)	1.0 (10)	–	–	–
Poland	1.4 (10)	–	–	–	–	–	–	–
Brazil	–	–	0.7 (10)	–	–	1.3 (10)	–	–
ASEAN-6	**0.6**	**0.4**	**0.3**	**0.3**	**0.6**	**0.8**	**1.0**	**...**
Total	53.3	43.6	30.3	33.9	41.9	46.2	57.3	75.6

ˣ Preliminary data ** in brackets – place
Source: Russian Federation Custom Statistics of Foreign Trade.

Table 11.3
Russia's Top Trading Partners by Turnover (US$ billion)

Countries	1997	1998	1999	2000	2001	2002	2003	2004ˣ
Germany	13.3 (1)	11.2 (1)	10.4 (1)	13.1 (1)	15.0 (1)	14.7 (1)	18.5 (1)	23.8 (1)
Belarus	9.2 (3)	9.3 (2)	7.0 (4)	9.3 (2)	9.2 (2)	9.9 (2)	12.5 (2)	17.6 (2)
Ukraine	11.2 (2)	8.9 (4)	7.3 (2)	8.6 (3)	9.1 (3)	9.1 (5)	12.0 (3)	16.8 (3)
Netherlands	5.8 (6)	4.9 (6)	4.4 (7)	5.1 (9)	5.5 (7)	8.3 (6)	9.9 (6)	16.7 (4)
Italy	6.2 (5)	5.0 (5)	5.0 (5)	8.5 (4)	9.1 (4)	9.6 (3)	10.9 (5)	15.4 (5)
China	5.3 (7)	4.4 (7)	4.4 (6)	6.1 (6)	7.5 (6)	9.2 (4)	11.5 (4)	15.0 (6)
USA	8.9 (4)	9.2 (3)	7.1 (3)	7.3 (5)	7.4 (5)	7.0 (7)	7.2 (7)	9.7 (7)
Turkey	–	–	–	–	–	–	–	8.7 (8)
Switzerland	–	–	3.7 (8)	–	–	–	–	8.4 (9)
Finland	4.7 (9)	–	3.4 (10)	–	–	–	–	8.2 (10)
Kazakhstan	5.2 (8)	3.8 (10)	–	4.5 (10)	4.8 (10)	–	–	8.1 (11)
Poland	–	–	–	5.2 (8)	5.2 (9)	5.0 (8)	6.3 (8)	8.0 (12)
U.K.	4.4 (10)	4.2 (8)	3.6 (9)	5.5 (7)	5.2 (8)	4.9 (9)	6.3 (9)	7.7 (13)
France	–	–	–	–	–	4.5 (10)	5.8 (10)	–
ASEAN-6	**1.6**	**0.9**	**1.2**	**1.5**	**1.7**	**2.2**	**2.5**	**...**
Total	139.4	114.9	103.2	137.0	141.9	152.4	190.7	257.1

ˣ Preliminary data ** in brackets – place
Source: Russian Federation Custom Statistics of Foreign Trade.

Table 11.4
Russia's Trade with ASEAN-6 (US$ million)

Countries	1996	1997	1998	1999	2000	2001	2002	2003
Exports								
Singapore	570.4	208.5	58.1	198.3	477.0	574.5	521.8	158.2
Malaysia	119.3	174.9	116.9	392.4	300.8	269.3	347.6	425.1
Vietnam	122.0	315.0	266.0	163.8	168.0	162.8	321.4	356.0
Philippines	143.7	123.6	33.4	73.4	50.1	46.2	97.8	184.0
Thailand	220.7	148.4	31.8	65.1	80.2	71.4	96.0	130.4
Indonesia	33.0	60.4	13.3	6.4	37.2	31.1	30.7	235.6
Total	1209.1	1030.8	519.5	899.4	1113.3	1155.3	1415.3	1489.3
Imports								
Thailand	54.1	105.1	61.2	98.0	89.8	107.1	227.3	301.1
Malaysia	48.0	120.2	122.9	84.6	87.4	161.5	230.1	300.0
Indonesia	102.5	118.0	89.1	50.9	70.9	96.1	162.5	182.7
Singapore	228.3	202.0	105.5	41.5	43.5	109.3	88.4	89.8
Vietnam	32.0	39.1	56.9	20.0	36.8	80.0	81.4	77.0
Philippines	11.5	9.6	8.6	3.9	8.3	22.1	30.8	38.5
Total	466.5	594.0	444.2	298.9	336.7	576.1	820.5	989.1
Turnover								
Malaysia	167.3	295.1	239.8	477.0	388.2	430.8	577.7	725.1
Singapore	798.7	410.5	163.6	239.8	520.5	683.8	610.2	248.0
Vietnam	154.0	354.1	322.9	183.8	204.8	242.8	402.8	433.0
Thailand	274.8	253.5	93.0	163.1	170.0	178.5	323.3	431.5
Indonesia	135.6	178.4	102.4	57.3	108.1	127.2	193.2	418.3
Philippines	155.2	133.2	42.0	77.3	58.4	68.3	128.6	222.5
Total	1675.6	1624.8	963.7	1198.3	1450.0	1731.4	2235.8	2478.4

Source: Russian Federation Custom Statistics of Foreign Trade.

sides. In any case, the Russian-Vietnamese bilateral trade increased to US$800 million last year and it is expected to reach US$1 billion in 2005.

Traditionally, among the founding members of ASEAN, Singapore has been the most important economic partner for the Soviet Union and later Russia, as a sea port, banking and transport logistics centre, popular shopping place particularly for "shuttle-traders" in electronic consumer goods, etc. Today it has largely lost its importance in the trading of electronic goods for Russians, as many items are now cheaper to buy in Moscow, for example, than in Singapore. But there are a number of other opportunities for the further expansion of bilateral economic ties, to be mentioned below.

In addition to low volumes of trade, another weak point in trade relations between Russia and members of ASEAN is their overdependence on only one or a few commodities.

For example, in 2003 more than 40 per cent of Russia's exports to Vietnam, 60 per cent to Thailand, more than 75 per cent to Malaysia and almost 85 per cent to Philippines were limited to ferrous metals, 65 per cent of Russia's export to Singapore represented mineral fuels, and 37 per cent of Russia's import from Indonesia consisted of animal and vegetable oils. A structure of this kind makes bilateral trade vulnerable to any fluctuations in the economic or political environment.

INVESTMENTS

So far there are only a few Russian investments in ASEAN economies and ASEAN investments in Russia. The accumulated amount of these investments was hardly above US$1 billion at the end of 2004. Perhaps the recent portfolio investment (with the estimated volume of US$300 million, December 2004) made by Temasek Holdings (Singapore) in Russia's telecommunication giant MTS is a good sign of new developments in investment flows between Russia and ASEAN. This is particularly important taking into account the investment activities of other East Asian countries in Russia including the already long experience of South Korean corporations, such as LG, Samsung, etc. doing business there; the increasing activities of Chinese companies in our economy (including in the area of information technologies); and a recent growth of interest among Japanese manufacturing corporations to investing in car assembling, wood processing, etc. in Russia.

REGIONAL ECONOMIC COOPERATION

Russia watches with close attention recent developments in the economic cooperation in East Asia, paying particular attention to the development of such regional mechanisms as AFTA, ASEAN+3 (APT), as well as to the prospects of ASEAN+China, ASEAN+Japan, ASEAN+South Korea and ASEAN+India free trade agreements (FTAs).

While Russia's economic interests in East Asia are for now concentrated in its North-Eastern part, we should watch closely the process of economic cooperation within the APT in order to be ready to use opportunities the emerging economic group can provide in the future for its neighbours such as Russia.

Following the decision to hold the first ASEAN-Russia Summit in 2005 in Malaysia, we may expect that it could eventually lead to a more active economic interaction between Russia and ASEAN as an economic group. But that will require effort on both sides to search for new channels of economic cooperation during the next stage in relations between Russia and ASEAN. In general, trade and investment flows between them are market-driven but governments should also provide assistance such as investment guarantee agreements (IGAs) for private business.

While acknowledging that FTAs have become a worldwide practice, as well as appreciating ideas to create one of them with Russia's participation, one should not underestimate the difficulties of negotiating such an agreement with Russia, particularly when our country does not have any experience of this kind and still has a number of obstacles to overcome in the process of joining WTO.

Nevertheless, starting to explore a possible free trade agreement between Russia and Singapore, which is probably the easiest country within ASEAN for Russia to negotiate such an agreement with, may be useful for reaching a wider agreement of a similar kind between Russia and ASEAN in the future.

FUTURE AREAS OF BILATERAL INTERESTS

While opportunities for development of Russia-ASEAN trade in commodities in the immediate future may be rather limited, many other areas of cooperation may look more promising. Among them are: Energy (joint research projects and joint-ventures in addition to simple trade practices); IT and biotechnology (joint research projects, mutual investments in production and services); general technological cooperation in various fields and forms; cooperation in transport, including establishment of land transport corridors, sea shipping and airline routes, etc; banking and financial services. Singapore can play an important role in developing cooperation in each of the above-mentioned areas.

Also Russia-Singapore cooperation in education and tourism may become of special importance representing a human dimension in the development of bilateral relations, particularly at a time when Russia and ASEAN have relatively limited information about each other. Promotion of tourism may be facilitated by putting several countries (two or three) in one tourist package. Singapore could then regain its place in Russian tourism that it has lost to Thailand, though one should point out that tourism to Thailand was considered to be only the sixteenth among the top twenty favourite destinations for Russian tourists in 2004.

Cooperation in education and tourism may lay a solid ground and establish a network for development of trade and exchange of investments between Russia and ASEAN.

ARMS TRADING AND MILITARY TECHNOLOGY COOPERATION

As Russia is searching for new markets for arms export outside China and India, we believe that Southeast Asia may provide limited but nevertheless important opportunities in that respect, particularly when there is a possibility of setting up production cooperation similar to what Russia and India, for example, are doing now.

Bearing this in mind, it should be underscored however, that the main efforts to enhance economic interaction between Russia and ASEAN have to be applied to the civilian part of their economies where the most opportunities exist.

Index